Systematic new product development

Schematic diagram of contents

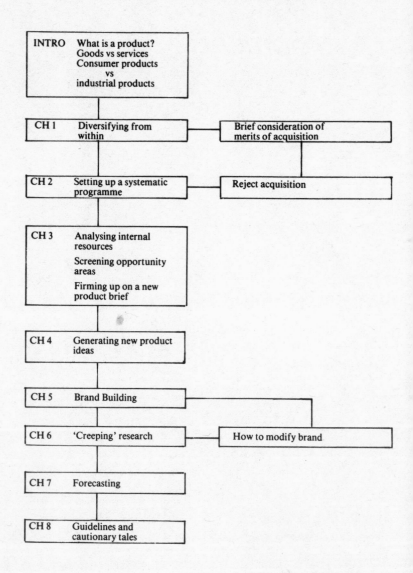

Systematic new product development

GORDON DOUGLAS, PHILIP KEMP
and JEREMY COOK

A HALSTED PRESS BOOK

JOHN WILEY & SONS
New York – Toronto

English language edition except USA and Canada published by
Associated Business Programmes Ltd
17 Buckingham Gate
London SW1

Published in USA and Canada by
Halsted Press, a Division of John Wiley & Sons Inc
New York

First published in 1978

Library of Congress Cataloging in Publication Data

Douglas, Gordon.
    New product development.

    "A Halsted Press book."
    1. New products.   2. Marketing.   3. Diversification
in industry.   I. Kemp, Philip, joint author.
II. Cook, Jeremy, joint author.   III. Title.
HF5415.125.D68.   1978   658.5'75   78-2398

ISBN 0-470-26328-8

© Gordon Douglas, Philip Kemp and Jeremy Cook 1978

Typeset by
Computacomp (UK) Ltd, Fort William, Scotland
Printed and bound in Great Britain by
A. Wheaton & Co, Ltd, Exeter

Contents

Introduction: What is new product development?

1. What is a product?

For our purposes, anything which requires marketing to anybody can be defined as 'a product'. The broadness of this definition is fully intentional. There is no essential distinction, in our terms, between developing a new brand of baked beans and a new package tour to the Seychelles. Both ventures require similar analytic, creative and marketing skills in their development; and both can be regarded as new *brands*. Throughout this book, therefore, we use the term 'product' to cover both goods and services, in the widest sense of each.

Such a definition is in no way revolutionary. The big travel companies, such as Thomson Holidays, have *product* managers in charge of (respectively) Greek Holidays, Spanish Holidays, Villa Holidays, and so on. The banks who introduced it refer to the Access credit card as a 'product'. The same term is used by insurance companies, referring to (say) a pension scheme for the self-employed. All such firms now talk of 'creating brands', and appoint brand managers to run them — just as companies such as Nestlé, Unilever and General Foods have always done.

The legendary days when, it is said, one could create a better mousetrap and see the world beat a path to one's door, have long gone (if indeed they ever were). Today, most new brands – goods or services – are developed with a target market in mind, and are usually subjected to some form of market research. The ultimate success of the product will depend on several factors: whether a consumer need has been accurately identified; if the product is correctly priced; to what degree the intended image has been communicated; and the reliability of any market research conducted on the concept prior to launch. All these marketing factors apply with equal force to a new brand of whisky or a new chain of laundromats, a new line in catfood or a new life insurance scheme. So does this book.

2. Consumer products and industrial products

Most of the examples in this book are drawn from the field of consumer products. But a systematic approach to new product development is equally valid for a new welding machine, a new combine harvester, a new design of hospital bed, a new polyester yarn, a new system of factory security, or a new generation of silicone chips – even though few, if any, individual consumers are likely to be in the target market for these products.

The analysis of a company's diversification potential, the method of searching for new product opportunities, the creative techniques employed in idea generation, and the system of 'brand building' (i.e. all the stages covered in the first five chapters of this book) apply equally to industrial and to consumer products. Only the methods of market research and sales forecasting (Chapters 6 and 7) will differ – and even then, only in methodology, not in approach. In our view, a systematic programme of developing new products is likely to be no less valuable to a maker of fibreboard for the building industry than to a manufacturer of breakfast cereals.

But whereas consumer product companies are, increasingly, seeing new products as fundamental to the progress of their business (witness the number of companies who now employ executives, or even whole departments, to concentrate solely upon new product development, as compared with, say, fifteen years ago), such dedication to new product development is still rare within firms who make industrial goods. In this aspect, at least, many industrial manufacturers have a lot to learn from their consumer-oriented counterparts.

Encouragingly, there are signs that many are learning fast. In drawing up their future marketing plans, industrial manufacturers are increasingly beginning to look beyond their dozen or so immediate customers (those firms, for example, to whom they sell their product for conversion into finished goods), and to consider the ultimate consumers of their output (the people who buy, wear or use those goods). Manufacturers of such 'primary' products as cartonboard, industrial fragrances, man-made fibres, or PVC, are now prepared to spend time and money studying the markets for the consumer goods which incorporate their products, or which do not as yet incorporate them, but might well do so. The information thus gained, plus any ideas for potential new products, can then help them to sell more effectively to the converters, their immediate customers; this process is sometimes known as 'back-selling'.

To illustrate what we mean, here are three specific examples:

2.1. Polyester yarn

The large firms such as Courtaulds and ICI, who make polyester yarn, sell the yarn to converters or weavers, who use it to manufacture fabrics. Some of these fabrics may be one hundred per cent polyester; more usually, though, they are mixtures of polyester and natural fibres, such as cotton, or polyester and other man-made fibres. The weavers sell their fabrics to clothing manufacturers; who in their turn sell the finished garments to such retail firms as Dorothy Perkins or Marks & Spencer; who sell to the public. (Even this is a slight over-simplification; we could also include in the chain those firms who do nothing but print fabrics.) Recently, the yarn manufacturers, looking beyond their traditional immediate customers, have tried to communicate directly with the consumer – to find out, for example, what characteristics are most wanted in a fibre, or what brand-names are memorable and acceptable.

Such brands as Tricel are the result of this policy. If Tricel can be shown to correspond to consumer needs and demands, then firms such as Marks & Spencer will begin to specify Tricel in their orders from the clothing manufacturers, who in turn will order fabric containing Tricel from the weavers, who will increase their orders of polyester yarn from the makers – in this case, Courtaulds. Thus a demand has been stimulated by working backwards along the selling chain.

2.2. Deodorant fragrances

Among the major manufacturers of fragrances, there have recently been considerable advances in the development of fragrances designed to combat unpleasant smells. Obviously, these have applications both for personal deodorants, and for in-home air-fresheners. Traditionally, these new fragrances would have been sold to the makers of toiletries and household products, who would then undertake new product programmes designed to create brands incorporating the fragrances. But, like their opposite numbers in the fabric industry, the fragrance companies increasingly talk directly to the consumer, and now undertake quite sophisticated market research among members of the public.

On occasions, this research has even taken the form of creating hypothetical new brands of deodorant, and obtaining from consumers a response to these new 'concepts'. Armed with these findings, the company can then approach their potential customers with a sales argument which, put crudely, runs:

> 'If you buy x tons of our new fragrance, you will be able to create brands of deodorant/air-freshener which will have distinct advantages over existing brands, and will enable you to increase your market share. Here's the proof — we actually created such a brand, complete with a name, pack design, and image. When we researched it, it did significantly better than all the other current brands.'

2.3. Instantisation technology

A certain company dealing in food technology had developed a superior method of 'instantising' foods and drinks. The firm had no manufacturing capability; nor had they any desire to diversify into the manufacture, sale or distribution of food and drink products. They preferred to license out their technologies to food companies. This new instantisation technology, though, proved very difficult to sell, despite having one significant advantage over all similar processes: it offered an extremely high level of solubility.

The company accordingly undertook a thorough review of the market for instant foods and drinks, and also generated several new product ideas, concentrating throughout on product fields where improved solubility would provide a particular consumer benefit. This exercise resulted in a shortlist of viable new product concepts (which included improved milk-shakes, jam-making products, wine and beer-making kits, and petfoods). With this list, the company found it far easier to sell their instantisation technology to food firms, who had been unable to see the potential of the new process until demonstrated in this way.

3. The scope of the book

By now, we hope, it will be abundantly clear that we regard new product development as being no less relevant to the industrial than to the consumer field; we therefore make no further apology for the fact that the great majority of examples we shall quote are drawn from consumer-product fields – since that, not surprisingly, is where most of our experience has occurred.

In broad terms, this book sets out to do three things. First, to explain why we believe new product development activity is crucial to the healthy survival of any and every commercial entity, no matter what the nature of its operation or (in the widest possible sense) products. Secondly, to show why we feel that a vast proportion of such activity as currently practised is, at best, wasteful and, at worst, completely wasted; and how a systematic approach can produce results that are better, cheaper, and far more reliable. Thirdly, to give the outlines of such an approach, citing examples wherever possible from our own experience in the field.

We have not intentionally set out to produce a do-it-yourself manual of new product development; though certain sections of our book may well be open to such use, and if so – well and good. Still less would we claim to be providing some kind of infallible rule-book of new product development. There *are* no infallible rules (or if there are, we have yet to discover them); if new product development *is* a science, it is as yet in its most sprawling infancy. What we *can* do – and all this book aims to do – is speak from our own experience, plus what we have read and learnt from that of others, and set down certain guidelines that we have found useful, in the hope that they will prove equally so to our readers.

1 Diversifying for the future

1. Planning for the next decade

It is the firms who start new product development programmes now who will be poised for successful expansion into new fields, and hence will stand to gain most if and when the climate of world business improves in the 1980s. (If it does not, of course, they should stand a better chance of survival, through having more strings to their bow.)

In some cases, the development of new products will be necessary for a firm just to stay where it is: faced with a declining market, or 'dying' brands, firms often resort to new product development as a means of staying in business. Sadly, the search for new product opportunities sometimes starts too late, the money for research and development runs out, and the new product drive is cut back before it has a chance of reviving the company's fortunes. But this is an error of problem diagnosis and of long-term planning, not of development. The more interesting observation is that, with determination and a little good luck, many companies *do* succeed in diversifying out of trouble, even in cases where the diversification programme may have started somewhat late in the day.

But being panicked into diversification is clearly not the best way to start – especially if new product development is a novel activity for the company. When should a firm think seriously about starting a new product development programme? One answer, of course, is that a firm should *always* be on the look out for new product opportunities, and *always* be studying the possibilities of entering new markets – especially those which are in some way related to its current activities, either by technology or marketing. Good examples of firms who operate virtually continuous new product development programmes are convenience food manufacturers such as Nestlé, United Biscuits, Batchelors, and Birds Eye. But it is unrealistic to expect smaller firms to operate non-stop diversification programmes, with executives permanently assigned to the new product development function. When should such firms as these start to think seriously about new product development?

2. Avoiding one-product dependence

Any firm which finds itself dependent for its future on the continuing success of a single brand should urgently embark on a search for new product opportunities. Just as a professional person – lawyer, accountant or marketing consultant – gets anxious if he finds he is becoming dependent for his living on a small group of clients (or still worse, upon a single client), so should a firm whose livelihood depends on the production and marketing of a single product line – no matter how successful – begin to worry. The situation may be more dangerous if it has come about insidiously, almost unobserved. A firm may once have been fully diversified; gradually, one successful line has come to account for all the company's growth. The trend has perhaps continued to the point where this product now represents well over half the company's turnover and profit. This is the time to think very seriously about further diversification.

The British firm of Whitworths is an interesting example. Originally local bakers in Northamptonshire, they developed a wide range of cereal-based products and baking aids. One of their new products was Weetabix, which grew to become brand leader in the entire UK breakfast cereals market. By the mid-sixties the Weetabix brand (a single line, with only two pack sizes) had grown to represent over three-quarters of Whitworths' turnover. Although the firm was supremely successful, and although the prospects for continued growth of the Weetabix brand — especially in export markets — looked encouraging, the company had the good judgment to spot the dangers of this excessive dependence on Weetabix. They therefore embarked upon a new product opportunities study, using the creative skills of their advertising agency to come up with ideas for new products.

The brief was to search for products which could utilise the strengths which the company already possessed in manufacturing and selling cereal-type products. The result was the successful brand Alpen, the first Swiss muesli-type product to sell outside chemists and specialist shops in Britain. A sceptic could, of course, ask: 'Why was a full-scale new product development programme necessary? Surely the opportunity was obvious, since the product is made up from a combination of ingredients (nuts, raisins, and cereals) already sold under the Weetabix or Whitworths brands? Shouldn't the company have been test-marketing new variants of breakfast cereal on a continuous basis?' Maybe, but at least Whitworths took effective action, and as a result dramatically increased their turnover, without any significant increase in overheads. At the same time they reduced their dependence upon a single brand.

3. Understanding product life cycles

In the days before marketing became a 'science', firms used to believe that their products would carry on selling virtually for ever. Provided that (i) the consumer still wanted the type of product in question and (ii) no competitor entered the market with a better version, a brand could be left to look after itself. In other words — to use modern marketing jargon — if the total market was expanding or at least static, and if competitive brands had no perceived performance or price advantage, then no specific marketing action — defensive or otherwise — was required.

However, in the sixties the theory that brands have *life cycles* began to gain ground. Roughly stated, this theory says that any brand, especially a fast-moving consumer good, has a limited 'life' — i.e. following a successful launch, it will increase its share of the market to a certain point, and then gradually start to decline, even if there are no dynamic changes within the market (e.g. new brands introduced) during this period. This 'life' is probably longer in markets such as shoe polish, or lavatory cleaners, than in others such as confectionery lines or children's ice-creams, and the length of this life can be prolonged by clever marketing activity and carefully timed re-launches, or drastically shortened by marketing mistakes or clever new product activity on the part of competitors; but nonetheless the brand's rise will inevitably be followed, eventually, by its fall.

How valid is the theory? Certainly old brands often die; but it is almost impossible to establish that their deaths were inevitable, given that virtually no market remains free from new activity (i.e. new brands, product improvements, re-launches, etc.) long enough for the theory to be properly tested. Also there are several classic cases in which the theory looks doubtful; that of Nescafé, for example, which suffered badly after the introduction of General Foods' brand Maxwell House. The latter rapidly built up a modern image of 'the young people's coffee', and Nescafé began to look old-fashioned by comparison. But Nestlé set about countering this situation, using a shrewd combination of marketing effort, product innovation, packaging improvements and advertising; and the image of Nescafé is now ahead of that of its rival on most counts.

From our point of view, it is particularly interesting that new product development was partly instrumental in rehabilitating Nescafé's image. The introduction of a premium-priced, high-quality 'sister brand', Nescafé Gold Blend, proved to have a beneficial effect on the image of the original brand.

The life cycle theorist, of course, might well argue that all that was achieved was to prolong, temporarily, the life of the Nescafé brand; and that, all else being equal, the Maxwell House brand still has the potential to 'outlive' Nescafé.

Another interesting case, which at first sight appears to disprove the life cycle theory, is that of Persil, the first ever soap powder. Four new 'generations' of washing powders have been launched since the days of soap powders: detergents, such as Tide and Surf; improved detergents such as Omo and Daz; biological powders such as Ariel; and non-ionic 'solvent' powders such as Drive. Yet, amazingly, Persil still remains brand leader in the UK – even though soap powders have been totally superseded in nearly every other country of the world. This would seem to result from a carefully-applied marketing and advertising strategy (the latter successfully overcoming any 'dated' image the brand might have been in danger of acquiring), plus a willingness on the part of the public to stick to a safe, well-tested formula in this particular product field.

Perhaps all that the life cycle theory really tells us is that an old brand, even though successful, is likely to have an old-fashioned image, and therefore is more vulnerable than an equally successful young brand. Hence more effort, ingenuity, investment in product improvement, and periodic re-launch activity is likely to be required (plus a greater risk of failure) than – all things being equal – in the case of a younger brand.

Whether or not one believes in product life cycles, the moral therefore is this: if the firm's main brands are old, and operating in markets where they are under threat from newer competitors, any attempt to re-launch or otherwise up-date the existing brands should be accompanied by a systematic new product development programme designed to search for new opportunities. At worst, such a programme should lead to new products which can take over as the old brands die; and at best the success of the new products will actually help the existing brands, either by rejuvenating the brand or house name (as happened with Nescafé); or by creating greater goodwill in the trade, and thus increasing distribution; or simply by bringing about economies of scale in production and administration, thus making it possible to reduce the price of the older brands, and hence keep them fit and alive a little longer.

4. Making investments in bad times

Most of the economies of the western world tend to suffer from fluctuations in demand, and from fluctuations in the investment climate. In the UK in particular, these 'stop-go' cycles have been particularly marked. When the economy is in recession, investment in new product development programmes is often cut back, in common with expenditure on advertising, public relations, market research and other marketing activities; yet in good times, when consumer demand is high, companies often neglect new product development in their rush to expand production and marketing resources for their existing products.

Given the inevitability of fluctuations in the national economy, our view is that the best time to start a new product development programme is during a recession for the following reasons:

4.1. Development takes time

A systematic study of new product opportunities, coupled with the selection of one or more viable new product ideas for development, need not take more than a few months. But the experience of companies in the packaged goods fields generally suggests that at least a year should be allowed for subsequent product development and testing. Thus, with luck, a firm which chooses to undertake product development in bad times will be ideally placed, with several development projects 'on the stocks', to take full advantage of the next predicted expansion in the economy. They may also benefit from their competitor's lack of activity during the slump, and his inability to catch up.

4.2. Development need not be expensive

It is quite normal, in times of recession, for even a medium-sized company to slash its advertising appropriation by anything from £100 000 to £250 000, probably accompanied by parallel savings in other areas. Yet new product development usually costs a mere fraction of such amounts. Ideas can be developed to the stage of 'prototype' brands and tested, stopping short of the eventual investment in new production plant; or a decision may be taken to progress only those ideas which do not require significant new investment of any kind – in which case the costs of new product development are limited to internal time costs, plus fees for market research or any other external specialist services.

4.3. Excellent use of slack resources

A cut-back in marketing activity is often accompanied by redundancies, or at least 'natural wastage' in staff. Yet rarely is the cut-back in staff proportionate to the cut-back in activity. This is not just because boards of directors are tender-minded on the question of redundancies, or wish to avoid redundancy payments, but also because they often genuinely want to keep a talented marketing team together, even at the risk of temporary over-manning. In the meantime, though, this talent can often find itself idle. What better use for it than for the company to embark on a systematic programme of new product development – either with the help of external consultants, or possibly with just the help of this book?

5. What about acquisition?

By now, it must be evident that we are concerned in this book with *internal* diversification – generating new products from within the company, building on existing strengths, assets and management skills. In other words, we are *not* talking about diversification by acquisition – whether it be successful take-overs which allow a company to move into new fields of activity, or mere asset-stripping ventures.

However, if only because acquisition is often put forward as a viable alternative to new product development, we feel it is worth spending the remainder of this chapter discussing the arguments for and against. Those of our readers who, for one reason or another, have ruled out acquisition as a possible line of action, or who feel the arguments pro and con are already familiar enough, may prefer to turn straight to Chapter 2, on page 26.

First, then, the attractions of acquisition.

5.1. A quick way in

There is no faster way into a new market than to acquire a firm which is already operating in the field. Nestlé, for example, having (for better or worse) taken a corporate decision to enter the frozen food market, achieved this ambition many years sooner by the acquisition of Findus, than had they set out to create a frozen food division from scratch.

5.2. Acquisition of new skills

Setting up a new frozen food division – even for a sophisticated food company such as Nestlé – would have entailed the acquisition of new skills – in frozen food processing, handling, marketing, and selling. By buying an existing company, these problems were bypassed. In the view of Nestlé's management, the purchase of a company already operating in the field represented a lower price of entry into the frozen food market than the investment entailed in employing new specialists and/or retraining existing personnel. Either way, of course, massive investment was necessary; which raises the question: 'Was frozen food the most logical diversification for Nestlé anyway? Were there not other new ventures which would have relied more on the company's existing strengths, and less on expensive outside expertise?' We discuss this general point in a subsequent section.

5.3. Instant distribution

Buying a company which already operates in the field chosen for diversification – even if the company is unprofitable – offers one immediate advantage: 'instant' distribution strength in the chosen field. Staying with the Nestlé-Findus case, this must have been a very important factor in the minds of Nestlé senior management. Obtaining distribution for a new brand of frozen food, in a situation where the frozen food cabinets in supermarkets are dominated by one or two large manufacturers, would have been (and still is) an extremely difficult task. The same principle holds true, to a greater or lesser degree, in many other product fields, from alcoholic drinks to household cleaning products.

5.4. Brand name potential

Buying a company immediately opens up opportunities for the wider use of the newly-acquired brand names. Family firms are prone to neglect the full potential of the brand names they possess (having failed to follow the system, advocated in this book, of searching for every possible opportunity for developing new products *within* the company's existing resources); they may thus end up on the take-over list of other, perhaps more entrepreneurial, firms who have spotted this potential. In some cases, such firms have been acquired, their factories and head office sold (this latter perhaps grossly undervalued) and their trading operation closed down, leaving the acquiring company not only with a small profit but also one or more valuable brand names from which to 'spin off' new products.

5.5. Rapid return

Finding companies whose assets outvalue the purchase price of their shares (not just because the value of a central London office has been underestimated – though this often comes into it) can be a highly profitable way to grow. The right injection of new management skills may lead to growth in sales (benefiting from the now larger company's increased selling muscle), while cost-savings in purchasing, administration and production may result from aggregation of resources, central purchasing and administration, merging of production units, etc. Hence really dramatic results can be achieved.

6. What's wrong with acquisition then?

Nonetheless, our advice to firms wishing to diversify is almost invariably: *create new products from within your internal resources rather than risk the problems of acquisition.* Why do we give this advice, and what *are* the problems of acquisition?

6.1. Few firms left to acquire

Shell, the Anglo-Dutch petrochemicals giant, has recently devoted considerable energy to the development of a business in household products. It has created a subsidiary company – Temana – which has developed from within the company a number of innovative products in the fields of air-freshening, household cleaning, household disposables, and even pet-care products. A faster way to growth, of course, would have been to acquire one or more existing firms in the household products field.

This strategy was at least considered by the company in their attempt to develop a viable business in Germany. But a survey revealed that there exist in Germany *only ten firms marketing household products which do not already belong to multinationals*, and all of these had been approached many times with a view to take-over. In many cases the companies were small family firms who were uninterested in selling out, as a matter of principle; and in other cases the price for the company was set absurdly high.

During the 1960s, in most European countries, investment analysts found little difficulty in spotting bargains for those clients with long shopping lists. This is no longer true, and acquisition can now be expensive; worse, like anything else which is expensive, it can often be a mistake. It is interesting to note that firms are tending to divest themselves of recent acquisitions − often after making a considerable loss on the initial investment. Examples of this are Reed in the UK, Nabisco in Germany, and the American food firm Grace − which made many seemingly random acquisitions of food firms (from pasta to jams) around Europe, and now apparently regrets having chosen this method of growth.

6.2. Unwanted responsibilities

Very rarely does acquisition take place for *all* of the apparently constructive reasons listed in Section 5. It is, for example, extremely unlikely that one finds a firm in a complementary area of business, up for sale, at a bargain price, with excellent distribution facilities in an area where the expanding firm is weak, with specialist skills and know-how which the expanding firm does not possess, and with strong brand names which the sleepy management have failed to exploit to the full. Instead, there is usually a single attraction which leads to a take-over (plus a lot of post-rationalisation about other advantages). Often, one hears such comments as: 'We never intended to get into manufacturing finished garments, but really it was a logical move, and when this firm was up for sale we grabbed it'; or 'We had to buy distribution to get into the alcoholic drinks market – so we bought this company. But we sold off all the bottling plant and the warehousing'; or 'What we wanted was a brand name to compete in the toilet soap market, so we bought this small firm making very expensive soaps – they even had the royal warrant – but we couldn't stand their management, so we did our best to pension them off or deploy them out of harm's way.'

This last comment poses an interesting paradox: that the ideal form of diversification in many cases – if only it were possible – would be to acquire successful brands, but not the companies and the responsibilities which go with them. All these comments, though, highlight a very real difficulty in the acquisition game: that of biting off more than the firm can chew. In the next three sections, we cover the three commonest forms this can take.

6.3. Labour problems

Closing of factories, with inevitable redundancies, frequently results from a take-over. But we should distinguish 'deliberate' redundancy from 'unfortunate' redundancy. Sometimes a company is acquired for its management skill, and its marketing strengths (especially distribution and brand name strengths), in the full knowledge that the inherited factory, plant and work force will be negative assets to be disposed of as soon as conveniently possible. In other cases, the take-over is accompanied by reassurances from the new management that no closure will occur; but the anticipated benefits of the acquisition may fail to materialise in the short term (possibly because of other difficulties mentioned in this section); and the inevitable factory closures follow.

A typical sequence of events in the latter case may run as follows: Company A successfully dominates the market in – say – paper tissue products. Company B has pioneered a new technology in non-woven fabric (a stronger, potentially more versatile, but much more expensive product with a smaller market and fewer uses – though a threat to paper tissue in the long term). Company B is short of capital, and has been struggling to promote the advantages of the new technology for some time. It is a technology which company A has not got and decides it wants for a combination of reasons – partly to seize future new product opportunities, and partly as a defensive measure, the company fearing that their traditional markets may be eroded. Hence an apparently successful take-over, celebrated by both sides. But then the opportunities for non-woven fabric fail to materialise; the larger investment in promoting the product fails to pay off; possibly a change in the economic climate causes sales of the more expensive fabric to decline slightly. The company looks for cost savings. Top of the list is the transfer of production of the non-woven fabric to company A's main factory, which was not totally up to capacity in the first place. Net result: company A has the technology it wanted – but at a price. Several hundred (or thousand) workers are out of a job through no fault of their own. At best, the company is in for some very bad publicity; at worst, for industrial unrest, strikes, sit-ins – all perhaps leading to further losses, and further redundancies.

'Asset-stripping' has acquired – perhaps deservedly – a bad name, thanks to the activities of certain wheeler-dealers. But acquisition which leads to the stripping of assets need not necessarily be bad. Take, for example, a regional confectionery company. Although brand leader in their area, they have not the resources to invest in the necessary advertising and sales force to sell their product nationally. A larger confectionery firm buys them out, sells off the factory to a firm in a different field who can make greater use of it, and makes the regional product to the same recipe, in its existing factory. The product is sold nationally, and sales increase several hundred per cent. Meanwhile the regional factory, given an intelligent re-training programme, is now employing all the old workers plus a lot more. All the original resources – the confectionery recipe, the brand name, both factories – have been re-distributed to everyone's advantage, and with a net gain to the national economy.

Unfortunately, such positive re-structuring rarely happens. Far more often a company, rather than think how it might best develop its own internal strengths, goes shopping, buys hastily and unwisely, finds its new purchase is proving to be a millstone – and at last reluctantly sells off the assets of the company it acquired (now, quite possibly, undervalued, because of the publicity resulting from the company's hesitations and difficulties). Everyone has lost; more workers are jobless; and the economy suffers.

6.4. Management problems

Another frequent result of take-overs and mergers is structural problems within the management ranks. To function properly, a manager needs clearly defined objectives, and a stable but stimulating environment. None of these conditions is met at a time of take-over or merger (except possibly the stimulation, which may be excessive). This applies to the managements of both firms concerned – except perhaps for a picked committee of managers whose task it is to implement the acquisition plan itself. It could be argued, of course, that an unsettled period is inevitable following a take-over, and that this is a small price to pay for the longer-term advantages. But the unsettled period often lasts far longer, and causes much more disruption and management conflict, than the take-over planners ever bargain for.

These problems are at their worst when the management styles of the two companies are fundamentally different. The company being taken over is often conservative, hierarchical, and unimaginative, but essentially straightforward and thorough in its management approach; whereas the acquiring company may be more entrepreneurial, ruthless, and risk-taking, with a much less rigid hierarchy, and a 'promotion by results' approach. Such a merger is very unlikely to succeed, especially if the tangible benefits prove slow to materialise. Often, the fiercest resentments may spring from seemingly trivial differences in management practice, as for example:

(a) Company B gives company cars to senior management; company A does not believe in management perks of any kind.
(b) Company A believes that the salaries of all staff should be published, based upon an American job-grading formula; company B has never heard of job-grading, and salaries are a closely-guarded secret.
(c) Company A operates an incentivised commission system for all product managers; company B has never even bothered to work out the profitability of individual brands.
(d) Company A operates a system of project teams who take collective responsibility for new ventures; in company B all new ventures have traditionally been the sole responsibility of the chairman.
(e) Company B operates a generous non-contributory pension; company A has no pension scheme to speak of.
(f) Company A pays exceptionally good salaries even to young managers who produce results; in company B salaries are mainly determined by length of service.

Such discrepancies are of course symptomatic of fundamental differences in business approach between the two companies – for example in the importance attached to marketing, the belief in the power of advertising, the advantages of computerisation in stock control, the belief in 'focused' factory systems, the value of shift working, the attitude to tax avoidance or even evasion, and the attitude to rewarding loyal customers. Yet, curiously, it is often easier to resolve these fundamental policy differences, than the more petty but far more personal problems which result from different pay structures, pension systems, and fringe benefits.

6.5. Limiting national economic growth

To allege that take-over policy can be partly responsible for limiting economic growth is a serious charge, and one which may seem difficult to substantiate – especially given examples of firms who have grown into major exporters through successful acquisition. But the true comparison is not growth via acquisition versus no growth; but growth via acquisition versus growth from within. If a firm in the milk business develops, entirely from its own resources, a successful business in chilled-cabinet dairy products (as did Unigate, under the invented St Ivel name), the market for chilled products, and hence the gross national product as a whole, will have grown; whereas if Unigate's growth had been achieved entirely by acquisition of an existing company in the chilled dairy products business, no net growth in the national economy would have been created. Of course, this argument contains two hefty assumptions: (i) that the success of the St Ivel brand was not in any way at the expense of competitors already operating in this field – an assumption which is only partly true; and (ii) that acquisition of an existing business would not have created *any* extra turnover – which is equally open to question.

Yet there is evidence that diversification from within a firm, when it succeeds, nearly always has the effect of creating products which *build on to* the existing market. The Mars group's entry into canned pet foods, for example, not only proved very successful, but virtually created a new market: existing firms in the business (mainly manufacturers of dog biscuits) scarcely suffered at all. It is interesting to note that the subsequent introduction of every new brand in this market – between 1950 and 1970 – had exactly the same effect: i.e. the new brands tended to build on to the existing market. There is also evidence (though we have never seen it systematically compiled or documented) that acquisitions are rarely successful enough to open up major new markets, or expand existing ones dramatically. When one firm takes over another, one plus one equals two more often than it equals three; whereas when a firm develops a new business from within its own resources, one (plus a systematic programme of new product development) can often equal two.

To take the argument to its logical conclusion: governments and government agencies, such as the British National Enterprise Board, should be less concerned with the re-structuring, re-grouping and merging of industry; rather, they should encourage new product development from within industry, and create a favourable investment climate for it.

6.6 *The vertical integration trap*

Finally, in this catalogue of the sins of acquisition, the danger of vertical integration must be mentioned. Take the case of a firm in the sausage business. Following, perhaps, principles similar to those outlined in this book, the firm diversifies into pre-wrapped bacon, pork pies, pork luncheon meat and even frankfurters — building on the strength of its brand name, and upon its skill and resources in distributing limited shelf life products. So far so good.

But where do the pig carcases come from? Probably from a variety of sources, with fluctuating quality and fluctuating prices. The apparent answer: first, take over a slaughtering firm, to ensure evenness of supply and uniformity of quality; and secondly, invest in pig farms, to ensure control over prices and over variety of pig. (It is a fact that a special breed of pig leads to a more economical sausage operation, even though this variety has few other uses.) Now what happens if the market declines, even slightly, or the firm loses one or two per cent brand share? Clearly the vast overheads of both the slaughtering and the pig breeding operations must now be shared over a smaller turnover, thus pushing up the cost of producing a pound of sausages. These extra costs must either reduce profits (thus restricting investment in necessary new plant, and — just as bad — in future new product development programmes), or the price to the consumer must go up. This immediately puts the firm at a disadvantage in relation to competitors who, unfettered by vertical integration, can now buy cheap carcases on the open market (where there is a glut due to the decline in the market for the end-product). This price increase results in loss of brand share, and so a vicious downward spiral sets in, its effects magnified at every stage by the burden of a vertically integrated system.

The advertising industry provides a further example; plunging enthusiastically into vertical integration in the late fifties and early sixties, it equally rapidly changed course in the seventies. It may come as a surprise to many people to discover that advertising agencies do not actually *make* advertisements: most of the studio production work connected with press advertisements (photography, layout, typesetting, etc.), and virtually all the shooting of television commercials, is sub-contracted to specialist companies. In the sixties, however, there was a fashion for agencies to expand into these fields via wholly-owned subsidiaries or specialist departments. These developments were not confined to the creative field; many advertising agencies formed or acquired market research companies, to avoid having to buy market research from outside sources, and to impress their clients with the full range of their in-depth service.

Unfortunately there are few industries which are so sensitive to small changes in the national economy and the climate of business opinion as is advertising. For example, in a year when the UK's gross national product declined by around one and a half per cent, the amount of money spent on advertising in real terms fell by well over ten per cent. Furthermore, the fortunes of individual firms may fluctuate dramatically and frequently – a single account can often represent twenty-five per cent of an advertising agency's billing, making the loss of such a client a catastrophic event. The advertising industry should therefore be the very last to take on the risks of vertical integration; and it is interesting now to see a new structure emerging, where any subsidiaries which still exist tend now to be *partly* owned, and run by managements who participate in their own profits. This allows the subsidiaries to compete in the open market in their respective fields, and means that the parent company has to enter into a normal contractual relationship (i.e. purchaser with supplier) with the subsidiary company on a project-by-project basis.

6.7. *Just plain unnecessary*

Besides the specific drawbacks to acquisition that we have listed, there is, in our opinion, a further over-riding argument: it is quite simply *unnecessary* as a means of growth. If a firm has a determination to diversify, coupled with some degree of entrepreneurial flair, and provided it follows a systematic approach to new product development, such as that outlined in this book, it can at the very least count on *some* degree of success; at best, it should prosper mightily. The same, as we have shown, can scarcely be said of an external acquisition policy.

2 A systematic approach to new product development

1. Most new products fail

It has been widely quoted (though no one, as far as we know, has traced the exact provenance of the figure) that eighty per cent of new brands on the market fail; in other words, the average company only succeeds in showing a profit on one out of every five products launched. If we accept this estimate, it certainly does not say much for the quality of most new product development as generally practised, and even if the eighty per cent failure rate is an exaggeration (though our observation suggests that it cannot be far from the truth), there are still few companies who can regard their product development record with much complacency – let alone pride. There remains ample room for improvement.

The conception, development and marketing of a new product requires, if it is to succeed, disciplined thinking and considerable attention to detail. (It also requires a good many other qualities, such as energy, enthusiasm, and an adequate financial investment; but for the moment these are beside our purpose.) In short, new product development is best approached systematically – which entails, among other things, treating all such apparently separate problems as branding, production, packaging, advertising, promotion, as related elements within the same process, best carried out either by the same specialised team, or at least by a closely-integrated group of experts with good internal communications.

To develop successful new products calls for skills and disciplines no less demanding (in fact we would say more so, but we may be biased) than those needed to run mature existing brands. And the acquisition, or development, of such skills is equally vital to a company's continued prosperity. Therefore, whether one applies the techniques oneself, or calls in experts, it is necessary to know in broad detail how such a system operates.

(The systematic approach, it is worth adding, offers a further incidental advantage. Besides being more efficient, it furnishes a framework within which each person can know just what needs doing, and by whom. Nothing is easier than to squander precious time and energy on misdirected initiatives, duplication of effort, and vast, floundering meetings at which everyone disputes over who does what next.)

2. Some causes of failure

2.1. Companies are badly organised for new product development

New product activity is like any other business activity: it will not organise itself; it requires careful thinking and a lot of determination to put the thinking into practice. It is almost certainly harder to get a new product off the ground than to maintain an existing brand. Existing brands have a certain momentum: they have customers; the sales force is used to them; the trade knows what to expect from them. Even if no one did anything for an established brand it would stagger on without undue hardship for a while.

A new brand, on the other hand, has no pedigree, and needs to overcome every kind of resistance – both active and passive – just to get started. The factory manager has no space on his production schedules; the sales force is busy with a key promotion on an existing brand; the trade has no shelf space left for new ventures. And all this is long before the consumer is let in on the act, and can decide whether to buy the brand at all.

Any company which plans to launch a new brand, therefore, needs all the energy and organisation it can muster. New brands are potentially very profitable, because they provide the company with turnover that it would not otherwise have had – often with minimal increase to overheads. But to achieve that turnover, the company needs to invest in an energetic programme. It should expect that getting a new product on to the market will absorb more of its energies, proportionately, than a mature brand. Yet most companies treat new products in exactly the opposite manner; it is the old brands that get all the manpower and effort; whilst new products are left to a small team which, all too often, never gets the backing of top management when the big push is required.

2.2. New product development is left to the end of the day

The chief daily concern of every company is its existing brands, and existing brands provide a varied and unending series of crises for their managers to unravel. Bad publicity, complaints from the trade, heavy competitive promotions, supply problems, labour disputes, a poor showing on Nielsen – all these issues always seem more important than the more distant and long-term problem of getting a potentially successful new brand on to the market. Nor is this surprising; existing brands provide the bread and butter. Therefore, any brand manager who has responsibility for both current brands and a new product programme will always – and who can blame him – put his existing brand work first.

Yet many companies still give new product responsibilities to managers of current brands, so in all these companies new product thinking is accordingly left to the end of the day. Only when the brand manager has solved his immediate problems, does he tackle his new product responsibilities; which is to say, he tackles them when he is tired and short of time.

Much the same is true of new product work carried out within (so-called) full-service advertising agencies. Few agencies include full-time new product specialists on their staff; instead, the new product work will be farmed out to this or that copywriter or executive, along with their responsibilities for on-going brands. The urgencies of getting a full-colour half-page for the existing brand into next Tuesday's *Mirror* will invariably take precedence over the less pressing concerns of new product work; the new brand gets such little time as is left over from the 'real' work of the day.

2.3. Inadequate briefing to outside specialists

One simple answer to the busy manager's time problem is: hire a specialist. If his own company does not have the time, or the infrastructure, to work out its new product development requirements, he can always call on outside help; indeed, most companies do just that. But not always with the successful results that the fat fees might seem to augur – and not always through any fault of the outside specialists, who may have been misleadingly briefed, or wrongly employed. For instance:

Piecemeal use. Instead of seeing the various specialist tasks as related, the company treats them all as separate, hiring a different specialist for each: this job for the advertising agency, this one for the research company; this one for the PR consultant, and so on. Everyone works very hard; a lot of separate problems are solved; the blind product test results are favourable; the commercial gets a high score in a theatre test (and with the chairman's wife); the sell-in goes well; the production line is running smoothly; the introductory promotion gets a high response; yet the brand fails.

'But we did everything' complain the management bitterly, vowing never to embroil themselves again in anything so ill-fated as new product development.

Appraisal vs optimisation. In briefing specialists, it is often not made clear whether the company requires to help to *optimise* or to *evaluate* a new product opportunity. Is the specialist expected to give the new product the best possible chance of success – by creating the right name, packaging, product formulation, design, and advertising approach – but without questioning the intention to launch? Or does the company want the specialist to assess the viability of the idea, and offer an opinion as to whether it should or should not be launched? Either brief is acceptable, but a confusion between the two – which often occurs – can lead to disaster.

3. Towards a systematic approach

The aim of this book is to show how new product development should be approached – not in a piecemeal way, but *systematically*.

We start right at the beginning: how does the company go about identifying and assessing its existing strengths (since it is on strength that the best new products are built)? Then we examine how these strengths form the springboards to idea generation. From the germ of an idea, we proceed to its development into a viable brand; the emphasis here is upon low-cost creative and research methods which allow ideas to be represented and tested realistically, modified as necessary, and retested until they are right. In conclusion, we show how a simple forecasting procedure can be used to check whether the final optimised brand is worth launching according to the company's sales requirements.

3.1. Analysing the company's existing strengths

We saw in Chapter 1 how companies often look outside when

they are considering diversification; they think first of acquisition rather than of internal development. And many companies start their product thinking, not by looking at themselves, but at their nearest rivals. Even if they are not actually planning to buy the competition, they often think no further than copying the competitor's ideas.

This means either a rush to get a 'me-too' product on to the market, or alternatively a refusal to consider an idea because other, larger firms have ignored it. For example, a few years ago about half a dozen food companies launched brands of 'make-a-meal', or skillet dinners (the kind of convenience dinner where the manufacturer provides everything except the meat), even though a study of the market potential should have warned them that there was room for only one profitable brand. Predictably, all the brands failed. On the other side of the coin are those companies who ignore markets because giants like Unilever or Beechams have not touched them. Yet Unilever and Beechams ignore many markets only because they set higher tonnage rates than other companies, but what is too small for Unilever is by no means too small for everyone else.

Much more profitable, we believe, is to look first at the company itself. What strengths has the company upon which it could build? Assets could include a strong brand name (like Homepride, or Cow & Gate); or a versatile technology (like the ability to fill aerosol cans, which prompted Johnson Wax to expand from polishes into anti-perspirants); or excess factory or machine capacity; or distribution strengths in certain trade sectors. In Chapter 3 we suggest a checklist of such strengths.

3.2. Opportunities built upon these strengths

Having identified the company's strengths, it is a finite task to make a list of the markets to which these strengths can be fitted. In practice, this generally comes down to one of two questions: 'How do we get into this market?', or 'In which markets can we utilise this technology?' In certain cases the company may even set itself the dual objective of getting into a particular market on the shoulders of a specific technology. Once an opportunity has been selected, a development brief must be written. We also discuss this in Chapter 3.

3.3. Idea generation

The important requirement here is for creative thinking, which can then be systematically applied − what might be defined as controlled lunacy. In many companies, for example, the idea of putting small mint ovoids in a plastic box, and selling them at several times the price of good old Polos, would have been written off as crazy. Treated seriously, and developed, it became the highly successful Tic Tac range of confectionery. A similar 'creative leap' took Showerings from unpromising 'sparkling perry' to the launch of Babycham.

We completely reject the belief that creativity and imagination are the preserve of a privileged few, nor do we believe that any attempt to describe the creative process, still less to structure it, will only serve to emasculate it. We aim at a system which allows *everyone* to have ideas, as many and as wild as you like; many wild ideas turn out to be winners. Little is lost by having a lot of bad ideas; a lot is lost by having no ideas at all. We discuss approaches to idea generation in Chapter 4.

3.4. Brand building

Consumers do not buy ideas, they buy brands. Therefore we need a system that allows the company to describe its new product ideas to the consumer in a realistic fashion. This means offering the consumer in research the closest approximation to a real brand. Most consumers hear about new brands from advertising, or word of mouth, or promotions, or shelf display. We can therefore describe new brands to them with mock advertisements, or press cuttings, or promotional leaflets, or packs. In Chapter 5 we describe some of the ways in which realistic, yet inexpensive stimuli can be produced.

Nor is the testing necessarily expensive. We can use flexible and relatively small-scale research to evaluate an idea; from that evaluation we can learn how to flesh out the idea in more detail; then we can retest; improve; and go on testing until we get it right. Chapter 6 describes some of the research methods we find useful.

3.5. Forecasting

There will come a time when the 'crunch' question has to be faced: will the new brand — now it is fully optimised — actually achieve a sufficient tonnage level to satisfy the company's profit objectives? We have developed a simple forecasting model, which uses data collected in the course of the programme, and puts them together in a formula which can be worked out with a pocket calculator in a few seconds. All this is spelled out in Chapter 7.

4. A recipe for success

We believe that most new products fail — and, as we have seen, most do — because they are not planned systematically. Lack of system leads to ill-defined objectives, a piecemeal use of expertise and techniques, and — all too often — a half-hearted and ill-fated product launch.

A systematic approach, such as that outlined in this chapter, and which forms the subject of this book, can largely minimise such risks. Brands planned and launched in a systematic way, we maintain, have a high chance of success.

3 Starting a new product development programme

1. Market orientation vs product orientation

There has been much discussion about the importance of greater market orientation in industry. Traditionally, most companies have been product-oriented; they tend to approach new product development along the lines of: 'This is what we can make: now how do we go about selling it?' By contrast, modern-minded companies are supposed to ask themselves: 'This is what, according to market research, our customers want: now how do we set about marketing it?'

Why is it that so many companies are still predominantly product-oriented, despite the evident wisdom of the market-oriented approach? Why do most marketing managers pay lip-service to the idea of creating new products to fit identified consumer needs; but in fact continue to prepare marketing plans and sales strategies for products created by their development department using the company's existing technology – products which are often no more than variants or line extensions of the company's existing brands?

One answer, we suspect, is that the market-oriented approach can be too broad. How does a company know where to start? Consider, for example, a firm making carpet shampoo which discovers, through market research, a gap in the market for a new type of carpet-cleaning appliance. What does it do about it? Patent and then sell the idea? Do a deal with an appliance manufacturer? Or make the investment needed to manufacture the new appliance, and then try to sell it – despite having no experience in the manufacturing and marketing of consumer durables? This case – an actual one – poses a real dilemma; and may explain why many companies claim to have tried the broad, bold market-oriented approach, only to abandon it on finding that new product ideas seldom get beyond the drawing-board.

The method which we advocate in this chapter – that of starting with a systematic analysis of the company's strengths – could be said to fall somewhere between market-orientation and product-orientation, and combine the best of the two approaches.

In analysing a company's technical strengths, the question, 'What can we do with our present technology?' will arise, and may lead to ideas ranging from minor variations on existing lines, through to new products in totally different fields which happen to exploit some aspect of the same technology. Meanwhile, in the course of analysing the company's *marketing* strengths, the question will come up 'Which new product fields should we look at?' Given a shortlist of candidate product fields, specific new product opportunities, based on consumer needs, can be identified within them; and the company can work out if, and how, it can make products to fit these needs.

In short, the effect of following the 'analysis of strengths' method is two-fold: first, to broaden the typical product-oriented approach; and secondly to narrow down and focus the market-oriented approach, by concentrating on a finite number of product fields which have been systematically selected.

2. Analysing the company's strengths

The first step in a systematic new product development programme, then, should be a thorough, perceptive and objective look at the company's existing strengths. Only from a detailed analysis of these strengths, assets and current resources can a true evaluation of the various opportunities open to the company be prepared. The aim is to find opportunities for new ventures which stem from these strengths – new products or services which represent logical diversifications on the grounds of marketing experience, technical skills or other assets which the company already possess.

The logic behind this approach is evident: by embarking upon new ventures which capitalise upon its existing resources, a company should be better placed to make a success of these ventures than another firm in a totally unrelated business. The proof of this statement must rest upon empirical observation – i.e. that in most cases it is true in practice – since, as so often in marketing science, absolute proof is difficult to establish: there are not enough cases where two manufacturers have launched identical new products at the same time, into a product field familiar to one manufacturer, but totally new to the other. However, we regard it as a safe enough assumption that a firm already in retailing (such as the John Lewis Partnership) would be likely to make a greater success of a new supermarket chain (as they did with Waitrose), than firms such as, say, the British Oxygen Company, or ICI, who are not in retailing at all; or that a firm in the travel business (such as Thomson Holidays) is more likely to succeed in organising business conferences and seminars than a firm whose experience is entirely in manufacturing, such as Kelloggs, for example, or Wall's Ice Cream.

2.1. Sticking to what one is good at

There are two reasons why a company which already operates in a related field is more likely to make a success of a new product venture: the product or service offered will usually be *better* – or *cheaper*. (Or, of course, both.) Better, because the company already has experience of the manufacturing process, or the problems likely to be encountered in marketing the product; and cheaper because they should be able to utilise some of their existing resources, thus reducing overheads, and effecting savings to their customers.

Thus prospects for increased turnover and profit through diversification seem to be greater by following the old maxim: stick to what you are good at. But it is essential to define this as broadly as possible: too narrow an interpretation of a company's strengths is likely to lead, at best, to line extension – i.e. new variants on existing products. It is therefore important to aim at an objective assessment of which business (or businesses) the firm is really in. Johnson Wax might be thought to be in the furniture care business, or more broadly, in the household products business; but following the development of aerosol furniture polish, they chose to define themselves as 'in the business of filling aerosol cans'. This led to the identification of personal deodorants, and subsequently toiletries in general, as logical areas for diversification – in which they have been successful. A more narrow definition of the company's business might have precluded this venture. In analysing a company's strengths, therefore, it is important to:

Be systematic. Otherwise some key aspect of the company's operation may be overlooked – it might perhaps be unique in possessing classified mail-order lists, or have special skills in handling limited shelf-life food products.

Be imaginative. Unless the analysis is carried out with imagination, and taking the broadest possible view, the more exciting new opportunities may be missed. For instance, in the Johnson Wax case, it took an open-minded approach to see the ability to fill aerosol cans as a key strength of the company.

So how, for example, would one define the business of a large brewing firm such as Watneys or Whitbread? At first sight, they are in the brewing business. Even this obvious observation opens up some new product possibilities: for example, the process of brewing beer is similar to the first stage in the process of whisky manufacture. Maybe whisky is a logical diversification? Upon further consideration maybe whisky is not so logical, as the water is probably wrong, the brewery cannot call its product Scotch unless it is situated north of the Border, and (probably being in a town centre) the brewery is unlikely to have the vast storage capacity required for maturing whisky up to ten years. Such considerations, though, should not be allowed to enter into the initial analysis of the company's strengths.

On studying Watneys or Whitbread further, however, one might draw quite different conclusions as to the business they are really in. For example:

The distribution business. The trend to centralised brewing, and the growth of the wines and spirits trade, has led to a situation where success is heavily dependent upon well-organised and cost-effective distribution. This way of looking at Watneys or Whitbreads could suggest that they should consider diversifying into the bulk haulage business – specifically, perhaps, the distribution of chemicals or other liquids.

The property business. The system of tied houses which operates in the UK means that brewing companies are landlords on a large scale: in some cases the property values of the pubs it owns represent more than half the brewery's total assets. Consequently, brewing firms have property valuation officers on their staff, they also have departments concerned with designing pub interiors, and experienced in contract purchasing of fittings. Maybe, with these skills, it makes sense for breweries to diversify into property generally; or into letting holiday homes; or into shop-fitting; or simply into interior design consultancy, thus hiving off the design department into a profitable sideline.

The leisure business. In competing for the public's custom, pubs are in competition with other forms of public entertainment. The sales of beer can be dramatically increased by the provision of jazz nights, drag shows, or simply one-armed bandits – even though the value of these entertainments must be weighed against the possible loss of loyal customers who just want a peaceful pint. Other entertainments, such as bar-billiards and darts, by contrast, do much to maintain customer loyalty, but can actually result in reduced total takings, as they limit the square footage of available space. All these factors are constantly under review by the marketing departments of brewing companies; as a result, a considerable amount of expertise has been built up in the entertainment field. This expertise could be relevant in other entertainments: sports events, amusement arcades, or even fund-raising events for charity.

2.2. Getting an objective view

Besides being thorough, systematic and imaginative, the study of a company's strengths should, above all, be objective. Boards of directors are notoriously bad at forming an unbiased view of their company's strengths and weaknesses. Middle managers may be in a better position to take an objective view. Outside consultants can often play an important role in such a study, either acting independently or as part of a project team. If the project team approach is followed, it may take one of the following forms:

Internal group. A project team made up of middle managers from different branches of the company's operations. The choice of a chairman is of key importance, since his task is to motivate the team into giving the project at least as much importance as their day-to-day departmental responsibilities.

Internal group plus outside consultants. The chairman of the group may bring outside consultants into the team – either professional marketing consultants, or representatives from the company's advertising agency, public relations firm, or market research company. The whole team may work together; or alternatively the outside consultants may be invited to present a separate report to the project team, who then use it as the basis for their full report.

Internal group chaired by an outside consultant. This can often be the best solution of all. The outside consultant brings the benefit of a fresh (and with luck, creative) mind to the problem; the fact that the chairman is an outsider may help to reduce internal politics within the group; and thus the members are encouraged to come up with more creative (and more wild) theories without fear of sounding crazy in front of a superior. Because the chairman is, theoretically, ignorant of the details of the company's operations, the members of the group are forced to explain every aspect of the company in considerable detail to him, and he can ask apparently naive questions without loss of face – the sort no middle manager in the company has dared to ask. This often leads to insights which might otherwise have been missed.

3. Following a check-list

Once the project team has been formed, the next step is to brief them. Typically, they may be asked to 'prepare an analysis of the company's strengths, with a view to determining the direction of our new product activities', or, even better: 'with a view to identifying specific areas for future new product planning', or even better still: 'with a view to selecting a number of new product opportunities for next year's new product development programme'. What help can we give to the team, who may well be undertaking an exercise of this type for the first time? Apart from our overall advice to be both systematic and creative in their approach, here is a suggested check-list of areas to be covered:

3.1. Manufacturing strengths

Does the company have manufacturing skills which are in short supply? Does it possess manufacturing plant which gives it a lead over competition? Is any of the plant under-utilised? Such key questions could (and should) have a major effect upon the company's new product development plans.

Indeed, these are in some ways the first and most obvious questions to consider, as any new product which can be easily manufactured using current machinery must surely have a headstart over other, more speculative, new product ventures. The invention of instant coffee is said to have been the result of (i) an idle spray-drying machine which should have been producing powdered milk, had the sales forecast been correct; and (ii) an imaginative technician who thought he would see what happened if he put black coffee through the machine.

Cow & Gate (the baby foods division of Unigate) provides a more recent example in a similar field: having excess spray-drying capacity, they set up a new product programme designed to identify opportunities for new products which (i) utilise the spray-drying machinery, (ii) make use of milk, the company's main raw material, and (iii) if possible fit its highly respected brand name Cow & Gate, with its serious, ethical, quality image. The result of the programme is the new product Vitarich, a milk drink for the older age groups, sold to the public through grocers and chemists, and to hospitals, where doctors have realised for some time that the feeding problems of geriatrics have a lot in common with those of babies.

A final example is that of a confectionery company, who realised that the chocolate moulding machine on which they produced Easter eggs was operative for only about four months of the year, and set out to find new ideas for chocolate products with an all-the-year round appeal.

So far as we know, they failed to find any successful products to fit this brief, learning quite early on that any egg-shaped chocolate confectionery automatically suggests Easter. But the *principle* they followed was sound; and, indeed, had they broadened the brief, and considered ideas for egg-shaped moulded objects outside the confectionery field altogether, they might even have come up with a successful idea.

3.2. Technological strengths

Does the company lead the field in any particular technology? Are there unexploited technologies the company possesses? These questions may be a highly fruitful source of ideas, but are often difficult to answer, as the value of a particular piece of technical know-how is not always immediately apparent, or can easily get forgotten – especially if no product has ever been created utilising the technology, or, even worse, when such a product *has* been created, and failed. (Take, for example, 'spotty' (or duophase) paint – paint containing two non-mixing colours, giving a 'random spots' effect when applied. The product, perhaps not surprisingly, failed dismally: but the technology is ingenious, and might still have potential.)

In many cases, firms may possess a particular technology without fully realising it. Another example from the paint field: a consultant was struck by the degree of know-how a paint manufacturer had in detergent technology. The method used to prevent brilliant white paint from yellowing (or at least to delay the yellowing process – since there *is* no perfect white paint) is identical to that used in blue detergents. This led to a new product idea: why not create a white paint with so much blue that it would actually *look* slightly blue, and use this fact as its 'unique selling proposition' and proof that it would stay whiter longer? The idea tested very well amongst consumers – do-it-yourself painters said they did not mind a slight blue tint for a few months after application, provided non-yellowing was guaranteed; but it proved too much for the conservative minds of the company's product development department, who had spent a lifetime working on how to get enough blue into a can of white paint *without* it being noticed.

Very often some incidental technological discovery is made in the course of research and development work on a quite different project. One hears a lot about such technological 'spin-offs' in connection with the American space programme (both electronic watches and cameras having benefitted in this regard, if their advertising is to be believed), but in the majority of cases these spin-offs are forgotten. In the course of developing a new washing product, one company found that it had inadvertently come up with a means of making one detergent liquid float on top of another one. Many years later, a scientist in the company's laboratory decided to explore the idea further; but market research indicated that a gimmick of this type had no place in the marketing of detergents for clothes or dishes, nor for shampoos. But the new product programme continued, and eventually a use for the technology was found in bath foams, where visual appeal and novelty are important.

3.3. Distribution strengths

By distribution strengths we mean two things: first, the ability of a company to get its products stocked by retailers – i.e. the power it has, through its size, its reputation, or the skill of its sales force, to influence retail distribution; and secondly the physical assets of distribution – deep-freeze lorries, chilled vans for fresh food, electric milk floats, liquid bulk carriers, or whatever. Strong distribution – in either sense – is an excellent basis for diversification, especially if both factors are combined – i.e. if a firm has the skill and influence to get new products into wide distribution via its own specialised distribution system. A certain firm has a fleet of vans (currently half-empty) delivering fresh meat pies and sausage rolls to grocers every day of the week. They are currently involved in a diversification programme into continental bread, rolls and pastries – a field in which several large food firms, possessing the marketing know-how but not the skill in handling limited shelf-life bakery products, have failed.

One advantage of developing new products to sell through the company's existing distribution system to regular outlets, is that it virtually guarantees that, be the product good or bad, the public will at least get a chance to try it; whereas the most brilliantly conceived new product will fail if a reasonable level of retail distribution cannot be achieved. A cautionary tale from the toiletries field: a new product had been painstakingly developed, and market research had indicated that ten per cent of the target market would become regular buyers of the new brand. The initial sales forecast, based upon this statistic, predicted a profitable success. But on launch, only *two* per cent of the target market became regular buyers; the product failed; and the market research was blamed for being wrong.

A post-mortem revealed that the product achieved only a twenty per cent weighted distribution (i.e. it could be found in only twenty per cent of shops, weighted by turnover). This wholly explained the brand's failure: the ten per cent of the target market who had said they would definitely buy the product did not expect to have to search for it from shop to shop; yet in real life eight out of ten of them would have had to do so. (For a justification of treating weighted distribution as equivalent to availability, see Chapter 7 on forecasting.) Thus the correct estimate of regular buyers was not ten per cent, but *a mere twenty per cent of ten per cent* – i.e. two per cent, which is exactly what was achieved. The original market research (implicitly assuming hundred per cent distribution) was therefore correct; the failure of the product was due to the company's inability to achieve a reasonable level of distribution; and the incorrect forecast was due to failure to take this into account.

The importance of distribution as a major factor in new product success is hard to overestimate. We recently came across a firm in the business of selling household disposables (e.g. aluminium foil, plastic bags and cling-film) through the grocery trade under a variety of brand names, who appointed a consultancy firm to search for new product opportunities. After conducting an 'analysis of strengths' (very much along the lines advocated in this chapter), they came to the conclusion that the company really had only one asset – their ability to sell successfully to grocers over the whole country. They had no powerful brand names, no unique management skills, no new technology up their sleeves, and certainly no strength in raw materials or factory handling (rather the contrary – they bought in many of their products from other manufacturers). So the brief was simple, though broad: 'What new products should we develop to be sold through grocery distribution, that are vaguely food-related?' Is this brief too broad? Not, we think, if the analysis of the company's strengths is correct – if they really possess *no* other strengths but their distribution system. Indeed, maybe it is too narrow: why stick to food-related products? This criterion was added, simply because without it the brief sounded somewhat naive: and, after all, the firm's current products were food-related, so perhaps it was best to stick to this area. Yet there seems no logical reason why a firm selling aluminium foil and plastic bags should find the market for, say, tea-caddies any easier to enter than the market for lavatory-brushes.

3.4. Management strengths

If the purchasing manager of a large food firm appears to have more interest in antique clocks than in fish-oil or cocoa beans, this is likely to be regarded by his colleagues as a weakness, rather than a strength. But why not diversify into antiques, using the knowledge and experience of the purchasing manager to develop this business as a profitable sideline? In reality, of course, the chances are that the purchasing manager's interest in antiques will not extend to running a business in them; and that the company's skills are far removed from specialised retailing of this type. But the basic principle is sound – to study the strengths of the existing management, even including skills they may possess which are totally unconnected with the business. After all, probably more diversification has taken place this way than any other, if one goes back to Victorian entrepreneurs who probably never heard of diversification. For small firms in particular, it occasionally pays to step back from the day-to-day running of the business, and take an objective view of what the management is really good at doing (and equally, of course, what it is not).

Of course, the difference, for a small privately owned firm, between diversification and just having a crack at a new business venture is a rather fine one, but even for a small company a new business venture should be selected with some reference to the talents of the individuals involved. We know of a small property company who came unstuck when they ventured into farmland and fruit growing; of a small printing firm who lost heavily when they tried to diversify into mail-order; and of service companies, such as management consultants, who have failed to make a success in manufacturing and selling.

Any survey of management strengths should thus include a no less realistic analysis of management weaknesses (which may also throw incidental light on current company failings). But negative thinking – however down-to-earth – should never be allowed to substitute for more positive attitudes. 'We're good at this, but we'd be absolutely hopeless at *that*,' is fine – but *only* on condition that it doesn't stop there, but always leads on to 'On the other hand, we could be absolutely marvellous at ...'.

3.5. Brand name strengths

Does the company possess brand names which are capable of being used, with success, in related (or even unrelated) fields? If so, which fields? Is there any risk of damage to the image of the existing brands, if these names are used in new fields? Which fields would cause the most damage? All of these questions can be answered by market research; since brand name strengths, unlike the other strengths discussed in this chapter, are objectively measurable. Brand image research can tell us how consumers currently view the company's brands; and concept testing can tell us how consumers react to the use of these names on new products (see Chapter 6 on research).

If analysis of a company's strengths — possibly backed up by brand image research — identifies a strong brand name, from which new products could be 'spun off', the first step is to draw up a candidate list of possible new fields in which the use of this brand name might give a headstart to a new product. This must be done largely on judgment and intuition, though market research can again help in pointing out possible directions. There is a simple research technique called 'brand personality research' — it involves asking consumers such questions as: 'If Sunlight were a person, what would he or she be like?' From this research (or from more traditional techniques) a list of associated words can be drawn up. For example, Sunlight is generally seen as traditional, pure, mild, fresh, lemony, versatile and yellow. These key words (which relate to the brand property Sunlight, rather than to a specific product such as Sunlight soap, or Sunlight washing up liquid) can often be extremely useful in suggesting new markets where the Sunlight name could help to gain an entry.

This process of identifying the characteristics of the company's brand names (or of the company name itself — e.g. Cadbury's or Dunhill), with a view to launching systematically-selected new products under these names, is often called *line extension*. This should be distinguished from mere *range extension* — i.e. creating further varieties under the same brand name *within the same product field*. Bringing out Players No 6 cigarettes in a king size version, or introducing a new flavour of Birds Eye frozen mousse, is range extension, not line extension; and though many of the same principles apply, we do not include range extension in our definition of diversification, since we feel it should be a constant activity, part of brand management.

There are basically only two principles of line extension: (i) use the existing brand name where it can add to the image of a new product; and (ii) make sure in doing so that the new product will not detract from the image of the original 'core' brand. For example, the Sunlight brand name might work well for a new soap powder; but Sunlight Lavatory Cleaner would certainly be a mistake, as it is doubtful how far the new product would benefit from its association with the 'core' brand, while the chance of damage to the existing Sunlight image is immense. This is an obvious example; but what about the less obvious? Were Cadbury's wise to use their name on instant mashed potato, not to mention canned soya products? Were Butlins right *not* to use the name Butlins on their new holiday ventures, ranging from cruisers on the Norfolk Broads to holiday villages in Devon and Cornwall? Were Spillers right to use the Homepride bakery name on a range of canned sauces? Such questions are perhaps best answered by the painstaking method of developing and testing alternatives; but this is a subject for our chapters on brand building and flexible research.

4. Screening markets

By now, the key strengths of the company have been identified; and there is a clear direction for the next steps of the systematic new product programme. But even after this analysis of strengths, a large number of options may still be open to the company. Take, for example, a firm in the toiletries field. They have identified their chemist distribution as a key strength, and so wish to create new products to sell through chemists. They have several strong brand names with hygiene and health connotations. One of the strengths of the management is its medical orientation, the managing director being an ex-GP and the marketing director having a degree in bio-chemistry. The field chosen for diversification is therefore: patent medicines, or new toiletries with health properties. A fairly precise new product brief; but still one which requires the examination of perhaps twenty or thirty candidate markets (medicated shampoos, cough medicines, analgesics, etc.) before the search for specific new product ideas can begin. Once again, we suggest a simple check-list.

4.1. How large is the market?

Could, say, a five per cent share of the market represent a profitable opportunity for a new brand? Or would the company need a thirty per cent share in order to achieve the minimum tonnage level below which the expense of developing and launching would not be justified?

4.2. What are the trends in the market?

Is the market expanding or declining? Is the trend to more expensive, added-value brands? Or is it becoming a commodity market, where brands are competing with each other on price alone? (Although fierce price competition generally indicates a market best avoided for new product development, the opposite may be true for a company which finds it has the skill to make a cheaper product.)

4.3. What scope is there for innovation?

A given market should not be ruled out simply because no immediate scope for new products is evident. Even so, it is important to make an initial judgement on how easy it would be to develop a product with a real point of difference over existing products in a particular market. Such judgements must be highly subjective; but still worth making, provided they are used to earmark certain markets as particularly promising – everything else being equal – rather than to rule out any options at this stage.

4.4. *The nature of the competition*

Is the market dominated by a single brand? Or are two or three brands fighting it out – often with heavy spending on advertising? Or is it a market with a large number of small brands – possibly regional in nature? Opportunities are particularly frequent in both the case of monopolies and multibrand markets. In both situations, a new brand with some genuine degree of innovation can make good headway; whereas a brand oligopoly – two or three brands competing – tends to be the most difficult for a new product, since the price of entry is usually high, with marketing expenditures being much greater. (This has been confirmed by the market research firm Nielsen, who have evidence built up over many years on the success rates of new products according to the competitive structure of the markets they enter.)

4.5. *What difficulties would the company encounter?*

The ideal market into which to launch a new product is one where the company has the technical skills, the factory capacity, a strong brand name, an excellent distribution system, and management talents to match. But in practice, all these factors are unlikely to be found together. Far more often, companies will be in the position of the aluminium foil and plastic bag manufacturer already referred to: that is, having only one real strength upon which to build. In these cases it is a worthwhile exercise to apply the checklist of strengths in reverse – to see how many of them represent difficulties which might be encountered in trying to enter particular markets. Against each candidate market, therefore, the company should ask: 'How important is our lack of a good brand name?' 'Does it matter that we haven't got distribution?' 'We'd need new technology – how likely are we to come up with it?'

5. Firming up on a new product development brief

By this point it should be possible to set down a clear and precise (though possibly still broad) new product development brief. The company's strengths have been analysed, and agreement reached on the general direction of the diversification programme; a list of candidate markets has been drawn up, with some ruled out as too small, too difficult to enter, or not right for the company; and some have been selected as being ripe for new product development and representing logical diversification areas. Now is the time to draw up a precise brief for the new product development team — either the firm's own new product development department, a specially-assembled project team, or an external firm of consultants. The ideal brief is neither too narrow nor too broad. Although it should be very simply stated, it should go into some detail on the reasons for selecting the particular market or markets for development, and on the analysis of the company strengths which led up to the brief.

A small European frozen-food firm provides a recent example of a 'model' new product development brief. The task the company set themselves was to create a range of exotic frozen savoury products to sell in individual tubs through supermarkets. The brief to the project team went on to explain, succinctly but in the necessary detail, the reasons for selecting this particular opportunity:

Why frozen food? Because the company, although originally and primarily an ice-cream manufacturer, had already achieved some considerable success in the frozen food field, and had built a strong, high-quality brand name.

Why tubs? Because the firm were expert in filling ice-cream tubs, and the fast-fill machinery they possessed, though currently under-utilised, represented one of their major assets.

Why savoury? Because the market for spreads, pastes, pâté and savoury mousse was expanding, though frozen food manufacturers were not represented in it. Dessert products, on the other hand, represented a static market with entrenched competition.

Why exotic? Because this would differentiate the new products from the mass of chilled-cabinet competition, and would help justify the price premium, which would almost certainly have to be charged for frozen products in this market.

Why individual portions? Because the country in question has a very high proportion of single-person households, who are heavy frozen food buyers; and because, even in larger households, there is a trend to single-person meals (the wife's lunch, the husband's lunchbox and the teenager's snack supper).

And why supermarkets – rather than small grocers, or home-freezer centres? Because this is where the firm's present distribution strength lies.

Given a precise, well-reasoned and detailed brief along these lines, the search for specific new product ideas can begin.

4   Having new product ideas

1. The need for originality

An analysis of successful new products has indicated that there are basically only two recipes for success: a price advantage, or some degree of originality. (See the Nielsen *Researcher* January-February 1970.) The most successful new products are often those which combine these two features. Classic examples of products which were once highly original, but which also had (or rapidly acquired) a price advantage over competition are: frozen peas (cheaper than fresh peas, more convenient, more consistent quality, sweeter, smaller); instant coffee (cheaper than coffee beans, more convenient); and washing-up liquid (cheaper than washing powder – which, incredible as it now seems, was formerly used for washing dishes – more convenient, pleasanter to use, and more efficient).

If an entrepreneur (having followed the advice of the previous chapter) has identified an opportunity for a new product priced below competition, and has the necessary technology to make it, then he can skip this chapter and go straight to the 'brand building' stage (Chapter 5). His problem is not how to create an original product, but how to put across the price advantage credibly, how to brand the product, how to package it, how to describe it, and how to advertise it – all different aspects of what we have termed brand building. Take for example, a chemical and pharmaceutical company, who recently found that they could make weedkiller and other garden chemicals at a price significantly below the brand leader and most other current brands. Having first identified the garden products market as justifying a major new product development programme, their next step was to find a distributor with skill and experience in selling to garden centres; then to create a brand name and packaging; and finally to launch the products nationally. Searching for an original idea was a part of the programme conspicuous by its absence.

But what about the rest of us, who wish to launch new products but without the help of a price advantage? Or those entrepreneurs who, even though their new products may have a price advantage, are still determined to add some originality?

At this point in the programme, the emphasis should be on *structured idea generation*. In other words, creative thinking (especially 'lateral thinking', following Edward de Bono's terminology) should be encouraged, but it is important not to stray too far from the problem in hand. (Or rather, it is important not to stray from the problem in hand by accident; deliberate 'excursions' away from the problem, with a view to returning to the brief with a fresh mind, are an accepted creative technique). Here follow eight different angles of approach, designed to add up to a programme of structured idea generation; but of course we would not claim that such a list can be exhaustive.

1.1. Finding a perceived performance advantage

No matter how cleverly a new product is marketed, there is no substitute for a genuine performance advantage. Whether it be food, detergents, domestic appliances, or do-it-yourself products, a research and development programme designed to create a product which the consumer will immediately recognise as superior is nearly always the best way to start, once the field for diversification has been selected. But such a programme should be accompanied by (i) an estimate of consumer dissatisfaction with current products; (ii) a realistic assessment of the chances of a demonstrably superior product emerging from the programme; and (iii) the realisation that the programme may not succeed, and that other avenues (e.g. a new image, new packaging, new method of use, new distribution system, etc.) should be explored in parallel. Throughout, it is essential to check via consumer research (usually simple product testing is all that is required) whether the advantages being built into the new product are noticed by the consumer. We have seen cases where much money and effort has been expended by a company in making an instant food product which is slightly more authentic in flavour; or in creating a detergent which tackles a particular type of stain more effectively; or in producing a new tea-bag which infuses faster; only to have these advantages go completely unnoticed by the consumer in 'blind' product testing. As in any development activity, therefore, effort and expenditure in creating a superior product must be weighed against the chances of success — which in turn will depend upon how satisfied consumers are with existing products, and what new technology the company can bring to bear on the problem.

But few technical development programmes end in total failure; and probably equally few end in unqualified success. What usually happens is that a product emerges from the programme which is superior in just one — often quite small — respect. In such cases (like the superior tea-bag) the marketing man has a choice: either launch the superior product — probably at a higher price — and try to draw consumers' attention to the product improvement; or forget the product improvement, and look for other ways into the market with a (probably cheaper) product which is, in performance terms, a me-too. A classic example of the success of the first option – even though a massive advertising budget was required – was the Procter and Gamble product Ariel. Ariel was tested by the Consumers' Association magazine *Which*, and the findings were that it has no advantages over competitive – and cheaper – washing powders *unless the product is used to pre-soak the clothes*; in which case its superior performance against protinaceous stains (wine, egg, blood, etc.) becomes apparent. But at the time of Ariel's launch, soaking was very much a minority (and declining) habit, being regarded as rather an old-fashioned method. Procter's solution was simple, though expensive: persuade consumers to buy Ariel, and use it for soaking; they then notice the better results, which they attribute not just to their changed washing method, but also (it is hoped) to the new product; this in turn leads to repeat purchase – even though they may soon forget soaking and revert to their former washing habits.

1.2. Hitting upon a new method of use

Many new products owe their success to the fact that they altered the normal method of use, or changed the way in which the consumer undertakes the task for which the new product is intended. This is true of paper handkerchiefs (no boiling, ironing); cleaner-polishes, such as Mr Sheen (no elbow-grease required); music centres (no wiring up separate hi-fi components); and instant tea (no messy tea leaves, no waiting to brew). We deliberately include instant tea in this list, as in terms of consumer trial (over seventy per cent of all housewives trying the Nestlé product Nestea within a few weeks of launch) the product was a huge success. The almost total lack of repeat purchase was due entirely to the fact that the product made an inferior cup of tea – rather than to any deep-seated resistance to the principle of instantised tea.

All these are examples of new products which have offered

greater convenience to the consumer – obviously a very important recipe for success in new product development. But not all changes in the method of use need be in the direction of making things easier. We have seen how Ariel succeeded in spite of, or perhaps because of, making the weekly washing task more complicated and difficult. A less extreme example: in looking for new opportunities in the market for window cleaning products, we conducted research which revealed that, apart from the twenty or so per cent of individuals who never clean their windows, households divide roughly fifty-fifty into the chamois-leather-plus-water brigade, and those who prefer a branded product such as Windolene or Ajax Window Cleaning Spray – which are used with a dry cloth. It emerged from the research that the main problem for those using a chamois leather and water was greasy windows, where water alone could not cope; whereas amongst those using a specialist product, the main dissatisfaction was smears caused by traces of the product left on the glass. Rather than create a new brand to compete with Ajax and Windolene, therefore, why not create a product specially for use *with* water and a leather – intended to appeal to half the market where there is no competition? We worked with a manufacturer to develop such a product, which tested exceptionally well. The test indicated that the idea would appeal strongly to users of leathers, as hoped; but users of branded products, too, seemed happy to revert to the more traditional method of window cleaning, now that it had been made more efficient.

1.3. More versatile or less versatile?

In searching for originality, one route is to make the new product more versatile – or just possibly much *less* versatile – than the brands in the market with which it will have to compete. Especially in household products, the consumer is always prepared to replace several products by a single one – provided that the new product adequately performs the jobs of the products it has replaced. Conversely, the consumer is always keen to try new specialist products if they seem to have a good reason for existing, and will continue to buy them if they significantly out-perform the general-purpose products on the market. Both avenues therefore offer opportunities for new product development; and both should be explored. Reverting to our window cleaner example: we could have developed, for instance, a product which also cleaned paintwork – allowing us to claim 'the first window cleaner which cleans the frames as well'; or we could, instead, have developed a window cleaning product specially designed for kitchen windows, where grease is a problem – thereby narrowing the usage of our product, but possibly strengthening its appeal.

Both approaches have their dangers, of course; and these can be checked out at the brand building stage. For example, excessive claims of versatility (the American product Grease Relief is sold for *all* grease problems, ranging from dirty collars and cuffs to car engines, and actually features a shirt in a frying-pan in its advertising) can cause consumers to reject the product as a joke. Taking a less extreme example in the same product field, we suspect that any new product – no matter how good – which claimed to wash both clothes and dishes, would fail if launched today, even though it is only a quarter of a century since a single product was universally used for both tasks.

The danger of over-specialisation is equally serious. No consumer wants to pay for, carry home, and find room for a large number of new products, if previously she made do with one – unless of course, the advantages are substantial. Research is therefore essential to check just *how* substantial such advantages, expressed in the most motivating way possible, are seen as being by the consumer. Also, the effect of a considerably narrowed target market or usage potential (as with our product for kitchen windows only) must be taken into account at the forecasting stage (see Chapter 7).

1.4. Making a more attractive product

We refer here to product (and packaging) *appearance*. This is an area where there is often great scope for innovation and originality, even when the product itself is no more than a me-too. In fields such as hi-fi and cameras, manufacturers increasingly realise the importance of design and styling of their products. Retailers often report of customers who buy a hi-fi system solely on its looks, rejecting the salesman's advice (and even sometimes the evidence of their own ears) that another, possibly even cheaper system is better. Traditionally, however, manufacturers have regarded the external appearance of a functional object such as a camera as of relatively minor importance – putting it after sharpness, reliability, ease of use, price, size, and weight as a development priority. And although attitudes are changing, it is only recently that many manufacturers of photographic and audio equipment have begun to conduct even the most fundamental market research on product design.

A good example – also from the field of consumer durables – of the value of creative design, coupled with the testing of alternatives, is provided by gas-fires – which for years were invariably upright, functional and unattractive. Their marketing, through Gas Board showrooms, largely took the form of advertising the heat output of the various models, expressed in BTUs – which few consumers could understand. Some simple market research was proposed; and it took only a few group discussions to show that consumers took the functional aspects of a gas-fire totally for granted, believing differences in performance or running-cost between types or brands were negligible. What they wanted – confirmed when a few simple drawings were introduced into the research – was an attractive piece of furniture to form the focal point of a room. And they were prepared to pay for it. Accordingly the first teak-surround gas-fire was marketed, incorporating an attractive shelf/mantlepiece, concealed controls, and a method of fitting to the wall. Even with a huge price premium over conventional models, it was a great success, and was rapidly followed by rivals.

But the importance of appearance as a factor in new product development is not confined to consumer durables. In food products, especially, a new product can succeed where another fails, purely on the strength of product appearance, or even pack design. A new range of dry pasta is being launched in the UK market, which, though of very high quality, has no notable advantage over similar products, and is to be sold at equivalent prices. In studying the opportunities for another new range, we conducted some market research which revealed an interesting finding: that consumers see bread, cereals, and even, to some extent, beer as being natural products, with all the goodness of healthy wheatfields; whereas pasta is seen as a factory-product, without much goodness, and certainly not 'natural' in the same way. Accordingly, this range is being launched with only one real difference over competition: packs which are extremely attractive, and communicate that the pasta is made solely from natural sun-ripened wheat. Time will tell whether these attractive pack designs, and the story they are intended to convey, will be sufficient to create a significant market share for a brand which lacks any other unique advantages.

(It is perhaps worth adding that we were precluded, in this case, from suggesting more fundamental improvements or modifications to the brand, since all the pasta is made in Italy, where the market is of course many times greater than in the UK. It would therefore have been uneconomic for the manufacturers to product specially-modified lines for such a tiny market.)

1.5. Looking for chinks in the armour

In searching for an original new product idea, a firm may often benefit from an imaginative look at the weaknesses of the competition, in the hope of finding 'a chink in their armour'.

Being responsive to public attitudes is part of this process of chink-spotting. The negative publicity which resulted from the revelation that nearly all pet-foods contained whale meat – at a time when whale conservation was becoming an issue – provided a tremendous opportunity for a new entrant into the market, with a range of products guaranteed to contain 'absolutely no whale meat'. (An opportunity which, so far as we know, was not in fact grasped.) Similarly, aerosols are currently receiving increasingly adverse attention in many countries; which offers many opportunities for new non-aerosol products – especially in the toiletries field.

1.6. Creating an original image

There are some fields where at least as much original thought should go into the creating of an image, as into the creation of the product itself. Cigarettes are perhaps the prime example; much the same is true of fragrances – perfume, cologne, aftershave, etc. One of the most successful products in the whole cosmetics/toiletries field in recent years has been Charlie, the range of perfumes and colognes from Revlon. The fragrance itself has some slightly unusual notes, and almost certainly a lot of creative thought went into developing it. But perhaps even more original thinking went into the image: a fragrance for an active, successful, liberated young woman who has a man's name (at least as a nick-name). At the time, an off-beat approach; but the number of its subsequent imitations testifies to its success.

Creating an interesting and motivating image for a new product does not necessarily involve anything out-of-the-ordinary or unusual. One of the most successful new product ventures we have been concerned with in recent years is the creation of a new brand of South African sherry – which, although of excellent quality, shares with Cyprus and British sherry something of a 'cheap substitute' image. After creating a large number of ideas for a new brand, one emerged from the brand building stage as a likely winner: the idea was to call the products Cavendish Cape Cream and Cavendish Cape Dry, to develop classically simple label designs, and to create the image of a traditionally British shipper – a family firm, Edward Cavendish and Sons – with links with the Cape.

There is nothing particularly new about the image of a British family in the sherry business (take, for example, Harvey's of Bristol); and certainly nothing startling about the choice of the name Cavendish. But the image was, in one sense, original – in that it enabled our brand to stand out in a class apart from other South African, Cyprus and British products; and, paradoxically, to do so by being not at all original in the world of sherry as a whole.

1.7. Searching for new points of purchase

We have already referred to Alpen, the successful brand of Swiss-type breakfast cereal launched by Weetabix (see Chapter 1). Alpen did not differ significantly from brands of muesli already on the market – except in that Alpen was sold in grocers, whereas the other brands were sold in chemists or health-food shops. Weetabix had used their distribution strengths to turn muesli into a mass-market product.

Other examples of this technique are selling do-it-yourself products and building materials through garden centres; selling garden products through do-it-yourself shops; launching a new brand of ice-cream, not through the traditional confectionery trade, but via a franchised-out system of ice-cream parlours; selling private-label paint in furniture stores; and offering a developing and printing service, plus free film, via mail order. We know of successful examples of all these moves.

The traditional distribution system should always be questioned, and alternatives, perhaps more original, should be considered at the idea generation stage of any new product programme.

1.8. Searching for new packaging formats

There are many ways in which packaging can create a point of difference for a new brand. It can be made easier to carry, lighter, more convenient to store, easier to open, easier to re-close, etc., than current brands on the market. Certainly no opportunity for such functional improvements should be lost. But packaging can be made to work for a new brand in ways other than strictly functional. Take, for example, the dried-milk product from Unigate, Five Pints. Its packaging (a plastic bottle shaped to resemble a milk bottle) immediately positions the product as an alternative to fresh milk, far more directly than products in cans or drums (such as Cadbury's Marvel). With the help of the brand name, the packaging also creates an impression of good value, and enables purchasers to work out exactly what they are paying for – which is far less easy with other brands of milk powder. It is too soon to tell whether Five Pints will ultimately succeed, although latest reports are highly promising; but it certainly deserves to.

The principle behind the above example is this: the new packaging, besides being novel in itself, serves as an integral part of the brand's function, purpose, and personality. Five Pints could have been sold in a plastic container resembling a tea-pot; this would have been more novel, but would have missed the point. To take another example: a successful new brand of tea-bags has been created for certain European countries, containing a limited range of expensive, speciality teas. The bags are not of the usual paper, but are made of muslin: a more expensive material, but one which (i) results in a better infusion; and (ii) is judged by consumers to be a natural and traditional material – thus helping to overcome the slight incongruity of a range of speciality teas being sold in bags in the first place. Thus the new packaging idea has been used not just to create novelty (which it does) but also (i) to provide a small product improvement, and (ii) to support the marketing concept. This is the line of thought to follow in searching for new packaging opportunities.

2. Aids to idea generation

Those who have read Edward de Bono's excellent books on lateral thinking will realise that coming up with new ideas involves breaking out of traditional thought patterns, and thinking *laterally*, not logically, about the problem in hand. But how does one set about applying lateral thinking to a particular problem? And how do you train people to think laterally? These are extremely difficult questions to answer. One might assume that the creative departments of advertising agencies – whose job it is to think laterally as part of their profession – would have a fund of techniques and training methods at their disposal. We know of a convenor of a senior executive business course who, making this naive assumption, wrote to several of London's top agencies, inviting them to provide a speaker to explain the creative process as practised in a large advertising agency. All the agencies declined; not because of any fear of revealing trade secrets, but because they felt that they would not have enough to say.

In this section, we discuss four specific approaches which we have found useful in new product idea generation, in the hope that they will prove useful to others.

2.1. Synectics and brainstorming techniques

'Brainstorming' is the name given to a group idea-generation session: the participants, who should be drawn from all the departments concerned with the development programme, indulge in focused idea-generation, while one member of the group takes notes. *Synectics* is a rather more structured version of brainstorming, and is the subject of a number of academic papers and a book by its inventor, the American George M. Prince.* Prince believes that all business meetings (except possibly those

---

* The Practice of Creativity, George M. Prince, Harper and Row, (New York and London 1970).

convened purely to transfer factual data) can benefit from the application of Synectic principles. Two of the main faults of business meetings, Prince demonstrates, from a study of American meetings tape-recorded and analysed in the 1960s, are: (i) reluctance of the participants to put up speculative ideas while in the presence of superiors; and (ii) good ideas being lost or rejected without a fair hearing. Synectics is basically a set of rules for meetings — especially relevant to new product development sessions, but worth taking seriously in any business meeting. The main rules are:

The spectrum policy. In reacting to any idea that has been put forward, participants must first find something (ideally *three* things) good about the idea, before they can criticise it in any way. Even then, the criticism must be put in a constructive way — i.e. 'What we need to concentrate on is how to cut manufacturing costs', rather than, 'That would be far too expensive to make'.

Assurance of effective communication. We all know how, in a typical business meeting, one may put forward an idea, only to receive a comment from another participant along the lines of 'interesting, but my idea is to … '. This is not only rude: it breaks another rule of Synectics: before any participant can enter the conversation, he must first indicate that he has understood the remarks of the previous speaker by paraphrasing them. This ensures that no idea is lost; the group must attempt to optimise it as far as they possibly can, before a totally new thought is allowed to enter the conversation. (The participant who is bubbling over with twenty or so wild ideas is encouraged to jot them down on a pad, and introduce them one by one as the session proceeds.)

Trained leader. To ensure that these rules are followed, a leader is appointed, who should have had experience in this type of session. He will *not* be the chairman of the meeting, and certainly not the person who has posed the new product development problem which the group is trying to solve. The leader does not comment upon the ideas, but has the responsibility of recording them, and of directing the meeting.

How useful is synectics to new product ideas generation? Having used the method, slightly modified, for some years, our conclusions are:

(a) it is more useful for problems where a single solution is required, than as a means of generating a large list of possible ideas in response to a broad brief;

(b) it is useful for especially intractable problems, but is usually unnecessary as the first line of attack;

(c) some of the disciplines involved, especially the assurance of effective communication and the spectrum policy, should be part of all business meetings. (Incidentally, we suspect that new product development meetings within typical British or European companies in the 1970s are more relaxed, and perhaps closer to the synectics ideal, than the American meetings analysed by Mr Prince in the 1960s.)

2.2. Gap Analysis

In trying to enter a new market, a firm should constantly be on the look-out for possible gaps in that market. The most obvious of these is a price gap — for example, no one is providing a suit of Saville Row quality at a Woolworth's price. Not surprisingly, price gaps are often very difficult to fill. Even so, it is worth looking hard at any market where the price differential between the most expensive (main) brand and the cheapest (main) brand is in the region of 2 to 1 or more — as this often indicates an opportunity for an in-between product, provided this gap has not already been filled. A classic example in the UK is the market for red fortified wine. At one end there is port, currently selling at £2 a bottle and upwards, at the other, British Rich Ruby, selling at £1 or so in discount stores. Curiously, there was no product in between. We have been successful in creating one — an imported fortified wine, close to port in character but not emanating from Portugal, priced mid-way between the two extremes.

Another example of successful gap analysis is villa holidays. Although small private firms had been offering 'self catering' holidays on a small scale for some time, only recently did the large package tour companies wake up to the fact that there was a gap in the holiday market – a segment of the public who did not want a total go-it-alone holiday, but disliked the regimentation of package tours. Further application of the gap analysis principle has led package tour firms to offer pre-booked self-drive holidays (take your own car, but no need to search for places to stay) – a 'product' designed to fill in the gap between villa holidays and total independence.

How should a firm set about gap analysis systematically? This is a problem, as we believe it is difficult to get good value from any *formal* gap-analysis system. Such systems do exist – in fact there is an elaborate market research technique which actually goes under the name Gap Analysis. Consumers are asked to rate all the brands in the market on a large battery of attitude scales (expensive/cheap, high quality/low quality, substantial/insubstantial, etc.); this data is then fed into a computer which proceeds to compare each scale with all the others in turn, looking for evidence of gaps in these two-dimensional 'maps' of existing brands. The main snag of this approach is that it is expensive, and takes up months of valuable time – during which several new product concepts could have been developed and tested. Another drawback of the technique is that it tends to come up with evidence for gaps which are either perfectly obvious (e.g. for an all-electric central heating system which is as cheap to run as a gas one); or for products which it is most improbable anyone would want anyway – e.g. for a fish-flavoured dog-food. As someone put it: 'There may be a gap in the market, but is there a market in the gap?'

Even when Gap Analysis *has* revealed a gap worth filling, one's not much further advanced, as the problem still remains of how that gap should best be filled; the obvious solution will not necessarily be the best. Had Gap Analysis been applied to methods of transport around 1850, it might have revealed: a fast, public system (the train); a slow, public system (the stage-coach); a slow, private system (the horse); and a gap for a fast, private system. Probable conclusion: breed a faster horse. The creative leap needed to invent the motor car would not have come from Gap Analysis.

2.3. Stealing other people's ideas

This may seem rather an unfair way to develop new products, and out of place in a relatively serious book of this type. Not so. Many of the best new product ideas have already been thought of, but they have not yet been exploited. Recently a firm organised a series of idea-generation sessions, with experts from all over the world, to come up with an improved packaging and dispensing principle for one of its international brands. The ideas were then shortlisted, and a search for any protective patents put in hand. To their horror the firm found that more than half the ideas – most of the best, in fact – had already been patented. Buying the rights to an invention is often cheaper than trying to get round the patent. It is also interesting to study the registers of brand names when trying to think up new product ideas. 'I wonder why they should bother to register *that* name in *that* field?' is a question worth asking, and might put the new product developer on to a new line of thinking, if nothing else. (It has been reliably reported that the total number of brand names registered in the English-speaking world exceeds the number of words in the English language.)

The best way, however, of stealing other people's ideas is to study foreign markets. What is happening in the USA, in Germany, or in Sweden in foods based on vegetable protein, or in computerised banking services, or in the development of do-it-yourself plumbing systems? Although it is possible that successful foreign ideas – especially American ones – will prove unacceptable to the British consumer, there is a good chance that they *will* succeed, if positioned correctly. There is certainly nothing to be lost by feeding such ideas into a new product development programme to see how well they research during the brand building stage. In fact, no serious programme of new product development should take place, without at least one member of the team having access to information – and the intelligent interpretation of it – on what is happening in other countries within the chosen product field.

Recently a small firm decided that processed vegetables would be a logical diversification, and proceeded to look for gaps in the market for canned vegetables. More exotic lines? Vegetables in special sauces? Mixed vegetables in a can? None of these avenues looked promising. By chance, one of the firm's executives happened to bring back a glass jar of vegetables from a business trip to Germany. (In Germany, Holland, and several other continental markets, quite a high proportion of processed vegetables are sold in glass.) The product in question was peas and carrots – packed together, in layers, in the glass jar; a fairly common combination on the continent, but little known in the UK. The company took the idea, and decided to develop it as a premium, speciality range.

2.4. Analogising from other product fields

The Synectics method, already described (pp 64–66), makes wide use of analogies as a means of encouraging lateral thinking. But good creative use of the analogy process can be made without recourse to formal Synectics sessions. We have already referred (Chapter 3) to the idea of white paint which is so white it has to look blue. This idea emerged from a thought process which went roughly: how is the problem of yellowing solved in other product fields? What about clothes? How do detergents do it? Isn't there some blue ingredient or other? This type of thinking can be applied almost infinitely to new product development problems;

even if it does not lead directly to a new product concept, it often allows manufacturers to view their product field from a fresh and unaccustomed perspective.

Even analogising *within* a product field may prove fruitful. In the next chapter (pp 97–8) we describe how we arrived at the concept of *Diners au Bain-Marie*; the key to success was transforming a new, and potentially suspect, cooking method (boil-in-bag) into an attractive proposition by analogising with a traditional, trusted method (bain-marie).

3. Use of market research to help idea generation

Without certain key facts and figures on the chosen market, it is difficult to set a precise new product development brief; and without a precise brief, much effort in generating ideas is wasted. But with the exception of this necessary background information, we strongly believe that market research is better used to check out new product ideas than to invent them. In our experience, most companies have a stack of research reports covering those markets in which they operate, or in which they may be interested; and a quick study of these reports, coupled with a few hours' creative thought, is a much better, faster, and cheaper way to progress a new product development programme than commissioning new research of the Gap Analysis variety. One can learn much more about consumer attitudes in the field of, say, sanitary protection by developing a few new product concepts and testing them at the brand building stage, than by any amount of so-called 'basic attitude' research.

There is a school of thought which believes that actual new product ideas can be generated by consumers in market research. This usually entails carrying out Synectic-style discussions, in which consumers are encouraged to have specific new product ideas. Proponents of such methods claim great success with them. However, we tend to rule them out because (i) they are more expensive than ordinary groups, since they need to last longer, and require particular expertise in carrying them out; and (ii) they are not guaranteed to be productive. (Even if they are productive, the crucial question is whether one could not have obtained as many, or more, good ideas by a cheaper method; and we believe that almost always one could.)

Most of the good ideas generated by this method turn out to be impractical, and most of the practical ideas to be obvious. This is mainly because the consumer does not have access to the company's marketing and production constraints, and might well be reluctant to consider them anyway. Consumers naturally have a different frame of reference from the manufacturer; they generally claim to want the cheapest, most reliable products, free of all 'unnecessary' trappings and frills. (These are not necessarily what they actually buy – otherwise 'own label' would have swept the field long ago.) Asking consumers to come up with actual product ideas is rather like asking a tax payer to draw up the next budget. On the whole, poachers do not make good game-keepers; at least, not on a temporary basis.

Although we rule out large-scale attitude research, Gap Analysis, or 'consumer-Synectics' sessions, there are two simple, fast and cheap research techniques which we find can often spark off creative thinking – especially in a field with which the new product team is unfamiliar. The techniques are (i) non-metric mapping – an established but little used method; and (ii) the detailed activity study – which is an approach of our own.

3.1. Non-metric mapping

If a computer is fed a table of distances between the major cities of Europe it can readily be programmed to print out the names of those towns in the form of a map. The map will show no coastline, and there will be no indication as to which direction is north, which south, and which east or west; but each town will, relative to the other towns, be in its correct position. Thus Newcastle will be fairly close to Edinburgh (perhaps in the lower left corner), and Athens not far from Istanbul (tucked away at the top right). Anyone with even the faintest idea of European geography will then be able to look at the map, realise that the top of the map is east and the left-hand side north, and, if he finds it more comfortable, rotate the map through 90°. He has thus interpreted the map.

It is possible, using this same programme, to feed the computer with information about different brands in a market, which it will duly print out as a map, indicating similarities and differences among the brands, and hence which brands are seen by consumers as competing with which.

To obtain the data is simple. All that is necessary is to get a sample of about fifty consumers to place the brands in the market (using photographs or packs to help jog their memories if necessary) in rank order of preference. Suppose, for example, we are considering the butter market. We confront our consumers with fifteen or so kinds of butter, including (let us say) English, Australian, New Zealand, Dutch, Danish, Normandy, Irish, and so on, and ask each person, 'Suppose you were shopping for butter, which would you buy? If that were not available, then which? And which next?' – right through the list. We end up with fifty lists of butter preference, which we feed into the computer.

Now these consumers have told us, not just which butter they prefer, but which they see as similar to which; since the second choice will generally be the nearest, or next best, thing to the favourite. At this stage, we ignore popularity; the computer concentrates on similarity/difference patterns. Say most consumers (as might well be the case) put Australian and New Zealand butter close together (whether first and second, midway, or last pair on their list), and Dutch quite far from both. The computer now prints out a 'map', on which Australian and New Zealand come close together, Dutch distant from both, and all the other butters placed according to the same system, averaged across the fifty lists. We now have a theoretical 'picture' of how consumers see the butter market.

What are the uses of this technique? Basically, it helps us to understand what is competing with what; and although it does not tell us why, it allows us to *theorise* why (just as we 'theorised' that the bottom of our geographical map was in fact west). It is thus a means of understanding what makes the market tick, and what any new brand is going to have to compete with — depending upon the positioning chosen for it — in order to succeed. At the same time it provides a simple form of gap analysis — for a fraction of the cost (and time) of the 'official' Gap Analysis research technique.

The weakness of this technique is also its strength. Non-metric mapping can never represent a definitive study of the market. Although we can be fairly certain that the map reflects a true picture of the way in which consumers see the brands in the market, there can be no proof that any interpretation of this picture is the correct one. But this makes it an ideal technique for sparking off creative thinking, while at the same time imposing a certain structure on this thinking. It is therefore a good way to start structured idea generation. (It also has the virture of being the only research technique which can help us understand consumer attitudes without asking a single attitude question, thus ensuring that the information obtained from the research is not just a reflection of the scales fed in.)

Here is an example of the technique in practice. We wanted to understand the dynamics of the cheese market in the UK, and accordingly conducted a non-metric map where we fed in a mixture of brands and types of cheese — both natural and processed (see Figure 4.1). We expected that the consumer would make a clear distinction between natural cheese and processed cheese, and between hard and soft cheeses. In fact neither of these dimensions seems to represent the main factors operating in the cheese market. Instead, if our interpretation (Figure 4.2) is correct, consumers seem to differentiate between cheeses in terms

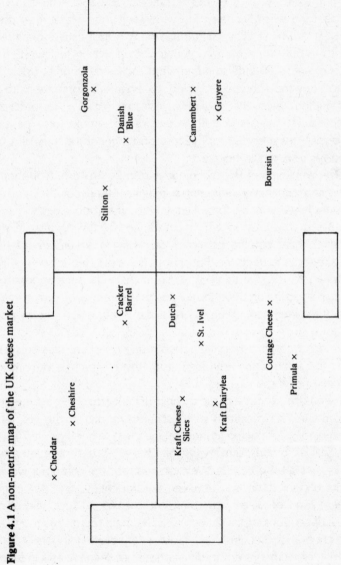

Figure 4.1 A non-metric map of the UK cheese market

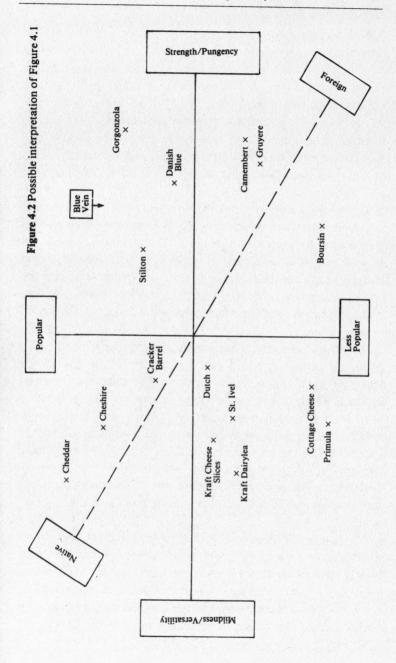

Figure 4.2 Possible interpretation of Figure 4.1

of how popular they are (the upright dimension); whether they are mild (and hence versatile) cheeses, or strong and pungent cheeses (the horizontal dimension); and to some extent whether they are native or foreign (top left equals native, bottom right tends to equal foreign). It is also interesting to note that Dutch cheese seems to come somewhere in the middle of the map – i.e. slightly foreign, quite popular, and reasonably mild and versatile; and that consumers have a very precise idea about blue-vein cheeses, grouping all three (Stilton, Gorgonzola and Danish Blue) close to each other.

These observations proved highly valuable in the subsequent development of new cheese concepts. But of course other theories to explain the map are possible. Disagreement about the interpretation can be almost as valuable as agreement in aiding the process of speculation and hence idea generation; and the risks of developing a new product idea on a false premise are not great, provided that the idea is properly tested at the brand building stage.

We have also used the non-metric mapping technique in fields as diverse as sausages and lavatory cleaners. In the case of the latter, we found that consumers make a clear distinction between products which can be used in the lavatory, but also have other uses (such as scouring powders, Jif, bleach and disinfectants) which occupy one side of the map, and products formulated specifically for the lavatory (e.g. Dot and Harpic), which occupy the opposite side. Block products (such as Blue Flush, Racasan, and Bloo) are located in an extreme corner of the map, suggesting that consumers do not see them as 'proper' lavatory cleaners at all.

The use of the technique in the sausage market was rather different. We were working with a firm which, at that time, sold twenty-two different sausage lines; but, as the map clearly showed us, the difference was not reflected in the minds of consumers, who found several of the lines indistinguishable from each other. By eliminating superfluous lines, we were able to cut the range down to ten; we then added three new, and distinctive, products to the slimmed-down range.

3.2. Detailed activity study

This technique is extremely simple, and takes little explaining. It consists of taking a very small sample of our target market — sometimes only ten or a dozen respondents — and asking them to keep a diary, for a few days or a week, covering every aspect of a particular task and how they tackled it. (The diary can be written or, even better, spoken into a tape-recorder while in action.) We have used this technique for washing-up, ironing, and make-up removal, and find it especially valuable in fields where the new product developer has no personal experience or insights — such as (in our case) baking cakes or industrial cleaning.

In the case of make-up removal, the diaries made fascinating reading. It is a field, we learnt, in which women feel very strongly about what they do. Some use only soap and water, insisting that special creams and lotions are a waste of time; others would never let a drop of water near their faces. However, amongst the mass of data we were struck by the widespread use of moisturising cream — by some women to remove make-up, and by others as the next step immediately after removing. This led to the development of a product which both cleanses and moisturises in one.

4. Imagination and common sense

In spite of all these aids to idea generation, there is ultimately no substitute for simple imagination, coupled with common sense. Laying down rules for the use of imagination and common sense as part of a new product development programme is clearly pointless. Instead, here is an example of a new product idea, which was created without the aid of any of the techniques listed in this chapter, and which can only be described as the result of combining these two qualities.

A study of air-freshener markets has revealed that in one country nearly two-thirds of all households have an air-freshener in their lavatory. The fact that many lavatories in the country in question are separate from the bathroom, and often lack outside windows, contributes to the need for such a product. Also, we found that people were direct and open about the need for such a product, without any of the embarrassment which the British show at the mention of nasty smells in the lavatory. The market for lavatory air-fresheners was dominated by aerosols, which had become something of a commodity market, with little brand loyalty, many 'own-label' brands, and the consumer buying on price. Yet our research revealed that most consumers hated aerosols – disliking the overpowering perfume, fearing explosions, and – more recently – aware of danger to lungs and to the environment. Here was an obvious opportunity to exploit a 'chink in the armour' of the products currently on the market.

But how could we create an air-freshener, which was not an aerosol, but still had the power to combat nasty smells quickly and at the touch of a button? (Or, rather, at the pull of a string – since most of the aerosols were designed to hang on a nail, and be pulled like a lavatory chain.) The company possessed a technology which seemed as if it might just provide an alternative: the ability to impregnate plastic with a perfume which is gradually released into the atmosphere. But the consumers did not want this slow-release type of air-freshener – as became evident from our first piece of consumer research. Aerosols might be nasty, but at least they were fast. So the problem became: how to turn slow-release into fast-release?

The beginnings of an answer came to us when we tried leaving some of the impregnated plastic in a briefcase overnight. Upon opening the case, a tremendous burst of perfume was released into the room. What was needed, therefore, was a briefcase to fit on the wall, which is opened and closed every time the toilet is used, releasing perfume-saturated air. Well, perhaps not a briefcase: just a box of some sort would do, provided it had a lid. From this thinking we developed the idea of a square container with a louvred front, controlled by a string like a Venetian blind. The box would contain the perfume-generating plastic, which would need replacing every two months or so. But this product would need to be rather bulky, and would almost certainly be sold through department stores — where the company had poor distribution — rather than through groceries.

How could the product be made less bulky? Perhaps we could use a motor, or some kind of pressure, to blow air past the perfume generator — but this led straight back to aerosols. What other forces were available? What about gravity? How about a cylinder containing the plastic, with a piston inside, which drops when the cylinder is inverted, forcing out perfume-laden air? Even better, why not fix it to the wall, with a suction cup and spindle, so it can be turned like an egg-timer? Even better still, why not make the piston into a plastic ball, made from the impregnated plastic, to be replaced every two months or so? And finally, why not make the cylinder transparent, so that the working of the air freshener can be turned into an attractive novelty?

This is a rather simplified, but hopefully not post-rationalised, version of the thought processes which led to a patented idea; and the only guideline which this case-history seems to exemplify is: use imagination plus common sense.

5 Brand building

1. Theory vs reality

1.1. Total realism – and its drawbacks

There is – theoretically, at least – an ideal way of testing a new product concept. You make a product, package it, and put it on a supermarket shelf in front of real live consumers – having given it the support and advertising, promotions, point-of-sale material, etc. This done, you then stand back and wait to see if the consumers will buy; and if, having bought, they will buy again. In short – you run a test market.

This method has one huge advantage over almost all other methods of testing: it gives you total realism. You are testing a real product in a real market – the acid test for any new product. Against this, of course, there is an equally huge drawback: it is an exceedingly expensive way of discovering that you have a failure on your hands. Not only is there the cost of manufacturing the product in sufficient quantity (which may well involve investment in new plant); there are also design and packaging costs; the cost of advertising, promotion, distribution, stock control; all compounded by the fact that, should the product fail, you will recoup less from actual sales, and possibly be left with surplus stock on your hands.

It is not our intention to knock test markets. They can be (and have been) criticised on various grounds: that they are not necessarily representative; that they are vulnerable to chance or deliberate sabotage; that they enable your bolder competitors to learn what you are up to, and jump the gun with a national launch. Such questions are outside the scope of this book. But in general we are happy to recommend a test market as a useful and logical step in the process of new product development – *provided it comes at the right stage in that process.*

In other words, given (as we have said) that a test market can be such a ridiculously expensive way of discovering that you have made a mistake, it should only be used when you are as certain as possible of having tested the product concept thoroughly beforehand, using far less expensive and more flexible techniques. In the course of the next two chapters, we will be outlining a number of such techniques that we have found useful – methods f representing and testing products prior to the major commitment of a test market.

But must the gain in cost-saving and flexibility imply a corresponding loss in realism? To some extent, yes. No testing method, however ingenious, can ever compete in sheer actuality with real products in real shops. But we maintain that it is possible – and highly desirable – to come very close to reality (or a skilful simulation of it) without vast expenditure; and this, too, is a theme that we will be developing at some length in the subsequent pages.

1.2. Special Offer – Concept Boards, 4p Off

Relatively few firms, these days, rush straight into test market – still less, into a national launch – without first undertaking some form of new product research. Which is all to the good, but raises the question: in what form is the (as yet non-existent) product to be represented, in order to research it? And this, we believe, is where quite a lot of new product development work can be faulted.

We have always been strong believers in realism when it comes to representing product concepts, for one basic reason: *consumers do not buy concepts, they buy brands.* In real life, consumers are not confronted with naked product concepts; they encounter them fully clothed, in the form of brands on the market, where they have no problem in evaluating them. But expose a group of consumers to a new product concept, *presented as such,* and your results will be (we believe) of very doubtful validity.

Put it another way: if you ask a theoretical question, you will get a theoretical answer. All too often, new product concepts are presented in theoretical form, by asking consumers (in effect): 'How would you feel if Bloggs Foods were to bring out a range of frozen soups, containing the following items, at such and such a price?' From which respondents will gather that these products do not exist, that in all probability they never will, or certainly not for a very long time, and that this is all a pleasant game of make-believe, without very much relation to reality – and in that spirit, they will answer.

Much the same, we think, applies to concept boards, which are so often used to represent new product ideas for research. (A concept board, for those unfamiliar with the device, generally takes the form of a board carrying a simple coloured drawing, and some hand-lettered copy; an advertisement in embryo, as it were.) For a concept board, no matter how neatly lettered-up, and prettily illustrated, is still only a theoretical question in the lightest of disguises. Concept boards do not appear in newspapers or magazines, or interrupt the programmes on television; no one expects to find concept boards on the shelves of their local supermarket. They are not *real.* And so the respondent, faced with one, still feels (consciously or unconsciously): 'This product doesn't exist. It's been dreamt up by some mad technician in a white coat. So it doesn't really matter too much what I say about it – I don't have to put my money where my mouth is.'

Why, then, is research like this still so widely practised? Perhaps for one simple reason: that it does get a response. Faced with theoretical questions or concept boards, respondents do not retort, rudely: 'Well, how the hell would I know? I can't tell from that – it's not real, is it? Give me a real can of soup, and I'll tell you fast enough if I'd buy it or not!' In some ways, it might be better if they did, but they do not – or not often, anyway. And since a response is elicited, it is assumed to be relevant.

A further danger is that most people like to be obliging – so long as it is no great trouble. Especially when assembled in a comfortable room, given coffee, and flatteringly asked their opinion by a sympathetic interviewer. Unless their feelings are very strongly negative, they will tend to be kind; it is not real anyway, so why discourage the poor chap who thought it up? Of course, the same problem must to some extent bedevil all research; but the less realistic the presentation, the greater the danger – or so we would maintain – of the kindly, misleading response.

1.3. Approaching the moment of truth

Under normal circumstances, consumers generally come across a new product in one of four ways. They may see an advertisement for it – on television, or in the press, or on a hoarding; they may read about it in the columns of a newspaper or magazine; they may hear about it by word of mouth; or they may find it in a shop. And any one of these may be the occasion of the purchase decision – that crucial moment of truth when the consumer decides to buy (or not to buy) something he or she has never bought before.

According to our philosophy, the closer all new product research can come to replicating that moment of decision, the more valid and reliable its findings will be. Therefore, we should always try to induce in consumers a frame of mind as similar as possible to that in which the actual purchase decision would be made. And to do this, we should aim to confront them with what appears to be a real product – presented in a form with which they are familiar, and can thus readily evaluate.

Ideally, the consumer should be made to feel that she is being asked to comment on a real, branded product which is actually on the market, or will be in the very near future – one which she may well encounter on her very next shopping trip. If we can achieve that, her response to the concept should be far more considered, more articulate, and more relevant to her real buying intentions, than if she found herself in an obviously theoretical situation.

All very well – but how do we work this psychological miracle? Let us revert for a moment to that list of a few paragraphs back – the four main ways in which a consumer may learn about a new product. Given that our new product does not, as yet, even exist, how many of these ways are potentially open to us?

Word of mouth we can rule out at once, since that is only likely to come from existing users of the product. Putting our product in the shops, perhaps the most crucial test of all, would be marvellous, if we could do it – but we cannot. (That, as we said, is the one huge advantage of the test market, for all its drawbacks.) But advertising, and write-ups in the press – can we not use these to clothe our ideas in a convincing semblance of reality?

The answer – not surprisingly – is 'yes, by all means'; and in the rest of this chapter we will describe some of those means, and how best to use them.

2. Clothing the concept

2.1. The simulation of reality

It is not in the least difficult to present a new product concept in such a way that it appears to be a genuine, fully-finished product. In fact, it is astoundingly easy. We do not claim any monopoly of skill or ingenuity for the techniques we employ in this area; and although we believe we pioneered several of them, there is nothing to stop anybody following our example, and doing just as well — or better.

Indeed, if most people do not do so, it can only be because they do not think it is necessary; or they believe such techniques to be difficult, time-consuming and expensive. In the preceding pages, we have tried to set out why we feel such simulations *are* necessary; we would now like to demonstrate various techniques for 'clothing' new product concepts in a realistic way, discussing the advantages and drawbacks of each, and showing that they can all be executed rapidly, effectively, and at a very moderate cost.

Before that, though, it is worth saying a little about the basic principles underlying the production of such realistic research stimuli.

In the first place, 'realistic' does not have to mean 'highly-finished'. There is no need to spend hundreds of pounds on elaborate pack design and expensive photography, in order to produce a believable stimulus for research. 'Good enough to look convincing — and no better' is the standard to aim for. Photography can work wonders. A blatantly botched-up pack, held together with bits of sticky tape, can look amazingly real when photographed by anyone competent enough to point a camera.

It is also sometimes believed that realistic stimuli cannot be produced until a concept is in a fairly advanced state — until, say, a brand name and pack format have been suggested, or even until a product has been produced. This is not true. As we will show, several of the techniques we use can be exploited at a very early stage of concept development, before anyone has more than the vaguest notion what the finished product might be like. In fact, such techniques can be especially valuable at these initial stages, and can save a lot of time and money in helping to rule out blind alleys of development.

Once created, these stimuli can be fed into any of the standard research techniques, such as depth interviews, group discussions, or (later in the programme) large-scale sample studies.

2.2. The white lie as a research tool

Inevitably, using techniques of this kind involves a certain degree of mild deception — or, to put it frankly, lying to respondents. (Persons of strict morality had perhaps better leave us at this point.) Since we are presenting non-existent products as being real brands on the market, the question must arise: 'Why haven't I seen it, then?' Luckily, there are all kinds of ways round this problem.

One solution is to say that the product is, at present, only on sale in another part of the country. Most consumers are vaguely aware of the existence of test markets, and so will find this credible. Also, anyone who has travelled round the country knows that the average grocery in, say, Yorkshire carries a host of lines totally foreign to shoppers in Surrey. So if the research is being conducted in Liverpool, one explains that the brand is only, as yet, on sale in Birmingham — and vice versa.

Another option is to attribute the product to another country altogether, but one where the language is the same (or similar). So in Britain a new product can be attributed to the USA or Canada, in France to Switzerland or Belgium, and so on. There are certain pitfalls to be avoided here, though. The stimulus has to be written in an appropriate national style, and allow for local spellings and linguistic differences (e.g. 'flavor' for 'flavour', or *'septante'* for *'soixante-dix'*).

Even more important, one has to bear in mind that certain product categories will incur a disproportionately bad (or, more rarely, good) image by appearing to emanate from certain countries. This is particularly true of food. The British, for example, have as low an opinion of American cooking (but not, oddly, of Canadian) as most other nations have of British. Equally, it is not advisable, when researching food products in the Flemish-speaking part of Belgium, to attribute anything to Holland, since Belgians profess to believe that the Dutch are a race of gastronomic illiterates who subsist entirely on peanut butter.

But on the whole, we have found that it is usually safe enough to rely on a fairly low level of consumer interest. Few consumers pay close attention to advertising (indeed, why should they?), or take much note of new products on the market. So if one says: 'Here's an ad for a new product that's just appeared; you may have seen it,' the reaction will generally be on the lines of: 'Oh, no, I don't think I've seen that one yet,' rather than: 'I've never heard of that; I don't believe it exists.'

(This might not always be true of certain highly-advertised product categories – most women would expect to have heard about, say, a new washing powder, and might be suspicious if confronted with an unfamiliar brand. But in most consumer fields, the principle holds good.)

In fact – though it is perhaps tempting fate to say so – out of all the hundreds of concepts we have tested by these methods, we have yet to have a single one disbelieved in. The concepts themselves have been criticised, of course – even sometimes derided – and the *execution* of the stimuli has not always been liked. But the criticism has always taken the form of: 'That's a badly-produced ad;' never: 'That's so badly done, it can't be genuine.' The idea of an advertisement, or a magazine article, not being 'real' just does not enter most people's minds – fortunately for us.

3. Tricks of the trade

3.1. *The press release*

By the term 'press release' we mean a piece of printed matter (almost always in black-and-white) which purports to be an extract from a newspaper or magazine – a news item or an article. It may be illustrated with photographs, or other visual material (such as line drawings); but its essential feature is that it pretends to originate from the columns of the publication itself, rather than from an advertisement.

As a research tool, the press release has a lot to be said for it. In the first place, it is extremely quick and cheap to produce. Once written, it can be ready for use in research within twenty-four hours – and then modified or amended, if necessary, equally quickly. Duplicates are no problem, either – you can turn out all you want on an ordinary photostat machine, for a few pence each.

Speed and economy are not the only advantages of the press release. It is an excellent method of testing several different concepts in one go – or several different approaches to the same concept. (To aid plausibility, each can be attributed to a different manufacturer – either using the names of real companies, or invented ones.) It is also – as we mentioned earlier – the ideal stimulus to use in the earliest stages of concept development, when the outlines of concepts are still vague, and there may still be several alternative approaches to choose between. The press release allows you to check out concepts in their most embryonic form, and rule out blind alleys of development, without further expenditure of time and trouble.

To illustrate these points, an actual example. Plate 1 is a press release we produced as part of an international project (already briefly referred to on page 5) for a food laboratory. The laboratory is connected with a chain of food marketing companies operating all over Europe, so we were testing our concepts in several countries. Our brief was to suggest potential applications for a recently-developed 'instantisation' technology, whose advantages (stated briefly) were very high solubility, and the possibility of producing instant versions of certain foodstuffs which had never before been satisfactorily instantised.

Given such a broad brief, we not surprisingly came up with a long list of possible concepts, which had to be cut down to a manageable number. This press release was part of that shortlisting process.

One possibility was instantised versions of dairy products – cheese, yoghurt, and even margarine (though not butter, for various technical reasons). But before we embarked on brand

EVERY WOMAN HER OWN DAIRY

Lisbet Brown tries making her own yoghurt and cheese.

MAYBE IT'S A reaction against our pampered, everything-on-tap age - or maybe it's in anticipation of the fancied austerity-to-come - but more and more people seem to be going back to making their own food and drink. Baking your own bread, brewing your own beer, vinting (is that the word?) your own wine - they're all on the increase.

Still, I'm willing to bet that, farmers' wives apart, very few women have so far tried making their own cheese - let alone their own yoghurt. Admittedly, until a week or so ago, nor had I - I'd always assumed you needed a well-equipped dairy, at the least, and preferably a cow or two. As indeed you did, until a firm called Wessex Dairies (based in Dorset, as you might guess) got into the act.

They've produced what they claim are the first-ever home yoghurt-making and cheese-making kits - no equipment needed, just a refrigerator. Taking the yoghurt-maker first (which is what I did): you add a teaspoon of the mixture (it comes as a rather knobbly powder) to a quarter pint of milk - or more in proportion, and mix it thoroughly. (They say hand-mixing is preferable, but electric's OK if you're feeling lazy.) Then you put it in a tray, and leave it in the fridge (not the freezing compartment) for about four hours. Take it out, stir it, add sugar if you want, back in the fridge for half an hour more - and it's ready.

So what did it taste like? Not at all bad, in my opinion. Perhaps not up to the original Bulgarian recipe - but

fully as good as any of the commercial yoghurts you can buy. A lot cheaper, of course - and none of those messy little plastic pots. And, in the packet, it'll keep indefinitely. So far, there's only the plain yoghurt available, but Wessex plan a whole range of flavours, with real fruit pieces in them.

And so to the cheese-maker. A little more complicated, this one, and you have to leave it in the fridge for at least 24 hours - but much the same basic method. So far, Wessex do three varieties: one to make a Cheddar-style cheese, one for cottage cheese, and one for a full-fat soft cheese of the Brie or Camembert sort. I tried my hand at all three, with very fair results.

The Cheddar was a little on the soft side, but with an excellent, very cheddar-y flavour. ("Not a bad old bit of mousetrap," said my husband, patronisingly.) My first batch of full-fat lacked a little of the true Camembert crust, but I tried, as Wessex suggest, leaving the next batch in the fridge for an extra day, and it was much better. The cottage cheese - no complaints at all.

All in all, then, well worth it - particularly given the cost-saving and increased keepability. Not to mention the delight of passing round the cheese-board with a casual "Made them all myself, you know..."

PS As I was completing this article, I had a triumphant phone call from Wessex - "We've just perfected our Margarine Maker." It's a pure vegetable fat product, apparently, which comes in powder form, you add milk (or water), mix, and leave it for three hours in the fridge. According to Wessex, four people out of five can't tell it from you-know-what.

Plate 1—A 'press release'

Plate 2—A 'semi-press release' (*Reproduced by kind permission of IPC Magazines Ltd.*)

Is your body wiser than your mind?

All living things – including ourselves – are in a constant process of growth and renewal. We never stop growing as long as we live.

But this growth occurs at different speeds at different times of our lives. When you're young, growth is astoundingly fast. Later, the rate slows down. As a result, the needs of our bodies change. The nourishment that was right for us early in life may not be so appropriate, later on. We may no longer need to eat and drink the same things – nor the same quantities.

Force of Habit

Our bodies realise this. But our minds – creatures of habit – may not. We go on trying to ingest the same things as always; then, noticing we don't relish them as we used to, think that we've 'lost our appetite', that perhaps we're ill. But we're not.

All that we need to do is re-think our diets to fit our changed requirements. Eat slightly different things – in different amounts – perhaps even at different times of day.

But above all, we shouldn't force ourselves to eat when we don't want to – just because we feel 'we ought to eat something'. There are other ways of keeping up our essential supplies of energy.

All the Essentials

One such way is called VITAL. It's a range of milk-based, high-protein drinks; and two glasses of VITAL contain all the essential vitamins and minerals to see you right through the day – even if you ate nothing else.

Even when your appetite's poor, you'll be able to enjoy VITAL. It's easy to assimilate, and tastes delicious. There are six flavours: Orange, Strawberry, Chocolate, Malted Milk, Coffee and Savoury.

VITAL comes in the form of freeze-dried granules, and can be made quickly and simply with either hot or cold milk. A jar of VITAL contains approximately enough for 16 half-pint glasses, and costs about 65p.

You can buy VITAL from chemists, and most good food stores.

Complete nourishment in a glass

Plate 3—A simple mock press advertisement

Taste the glory of Greece in a glass of Hellenic Wine

For three thousand years and more, the Greeks have been producing wine. And from Cleopatra to Lord Byron, there's been no lack of testimonials to the excellence of the wines of Greece.

Hellenic Wines – like the people of Greece themselves – are many and varied. Some, like the delicate white Glafkos from the island of Kos, deserve to be sipped and savoured. Others, such as the forthright red Romeiko of Crete make the ideal robust accompaniment to Greek food – or to steak, goulash, or even a curry.

There's Bryon's favourite, the sweet white Samian. Mavrodaphne, dark, strong, and beautiful as its name. Tangy Retsina – a taste well worth acquiring. And many more . . .

Pour yourself a glass of Hellenic Wine today. You'll be in excellent company.

HELLENIC WINE
The glory of Greece

Plate 4—A mock press ad incorporating scrap art

Lancaster—when you're with people you like.

Plate 5—A mock press ad with finished pack design

Drings
Luxury Sausages.

For when you run out of venison.

Our Luxury Sausages won't be for everybody.
They're not cheap, for a start. Their flavours
are unfashionably self-assertive. And we shan't be
making them in very large quantities.

Partly because the meats we put in our Luxury Sausages
tend to be in short supply; but mainly because
a lot of old-fashioned care goes into the making
of them. And old-fashioned care isn't
something you rush.

So you may have to hunt around a bit for our
Luxury Sausages. But never mind; it'll give you an
even better appetite.

Venison Sausages. Deer, but worth it. **Game Sausages.** For the high life. **Duck Sausages.** Worth going out for. **Ptarmigan Sausages.** Pticularly ptasty. **Hare Sausages.** Hare today – gone tomorrow. **Lamb Sausages.** Byron would've loved them. **Boar Sausages.** You'll be wild about them.

Drings Luxury Sausages

Plate 6—A mock press ad incorporating original
photography

Plate 7—A mock press ad combining rough pack design
    with line drawing

Plate 8—A poster site . . .

Plate 9—. . . transformed

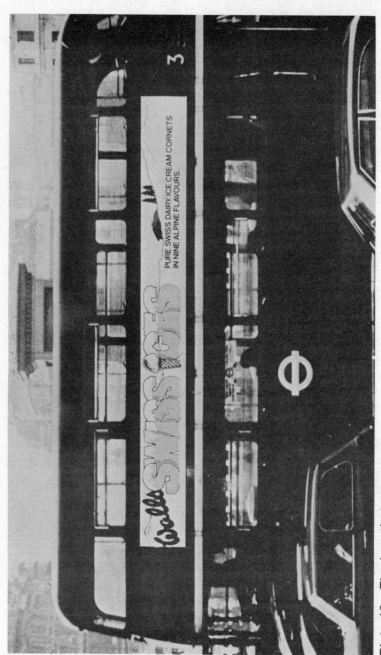

Plate 10—The bus that never was

building – deciding on brand names, pack designs, and so on – it seemed worth getting answers to some rather more basic questions.

For a start, would consumers even consider such an outlandish concept as 'instant cheese', or was it a contradiction in terms – an unnatural interference with a very natural food? Should we attempt to counter such a feeling by giving fairly elaborate making-up instructions? How 'instant' should it be – would people rather wait for it to be ready, and if so, how long? Would consumers prefer to reconstitute the products with milk, rather than with water? Would attitudes to 'instant yoghurt' and to 'instant cheese' be similar, or not? Would consumers rather add their own fruit to the yoghurt mix, or have it ready included? If the 'cheese' came out a little soft – as seemed likely – would this be a major negative? Which types of 'cheese' – if any – would people like to make? Was 'instant margarine' even worth considering? And so on.

All these variables we built into the text of our press release. It was written, and laid out, in the style of *Nova* magazine (now, alas, defunct), whose readership, we felt, would be fairly representative of the market sector such products might be aimed at.

In research, all our questions were answered. Making one's own cheese, we learnt, was a very attractive proposition. That it should take a day or two to make seemed quite acceptable – it was a natural process, after all, and not to be hurried. A literally 'instant' cheese would be a contradiction in terms. Cheddar, in Britain at any rate, was not surprisingly the most popular cheese to make – if it came out too soft, that would be a slight drawback, but the flavour was the main thing. There was no great enthusiasm for cottage cheese (a pity, since that would have come out best with this process). But respondents reacted with enthusiasm to the thought of showing-off with one's own home-made cheeses – a useful hint as to how we might angle any eventual advertising.

The other two concepts were not so successful. Yoghurt, it seems, is no longer thought of as a natural product – nowadays it is churned out in huge factories and put in plastic pots. To succeed, our product would need to be totally 'instant' — no one is going to wait four hours, if the kids are clamouring for yoghurt, they want it *now!* As for making your own margarine — no way. Margarine is a totally artificial substance; who would want to make their own?

So from one press release we had learnt: that instant margarine certainly was not worth pursuing; that instant yoghurt did not have much going for it; but that instantised cheese offered distinct possibilities, if positioned correctly — and we had gained some clear indications how that might be done. A good deal of valuable information, from one simple, inexpensive stimulus.

Our example also demonstrates a further advantage of the press release technique: thanks to its supposed impartiality, it provides an excellent way of checking out potential negatives in concepts. An advertisement, by its very nature, can only praise the products it features. But a press release is — supposedly — the work of an independent journalist, and so can quite credibly raise critical points, as in this case, where 'Lisbet Brown' mentions that the Cheddar she made was 'a little on the soft side'. We knew that this was a probable weakness in the product — but was it a serious one, in the eyes of consumers? From our research, it seemed that it was not. But in the context of an advertisement, it would have been difficult to raise such a point.

Sometimes, when we have had grave doubts about a certain concept, we have even produced a totally hostile press release, furiously attacking our own idea. This we regard as the acid test; if consumers, even with the moral support of what they take to be an independent journalist, still regard our concept favourably, and dismiss the criticism as unimportant or irrelevant — we think we are justified in pursuing the idea further. (If they agree with the hostile 'journalist', of course — well, we have problems, but at least we have indentified the danger zone.)

When we first began using press releases, we often used to 'fake' them back into a page or an issue of the magazine they were supposed to come from. This certainly added to the realism of the technique. We could hand round copies of a genuine magazine to respondents, saying 'If you'll just turn to page 38, there's an article there we'd like your comments on.' But the trick had its dangers. It could have occured that one respondent in a group might have looked up, puzzled or suspicious, and said: 'That's odd – I *always* read the *Molestranglers' Monthly*, and I don't recall seeing *this* article in it. ...' Fortunately, this disaster never occurred; but it might have done, and we decided it was not worth the risk. Nowadays we simply have the article written and type-set in the style of this or that magazine, and shown to respondents in limbo, on an otherwise blank sheet, with some such remark as 'Here's a piece we cut out of a recent magazine, and had copied.' (In the unlikely event that a respondent asks which magazine it is from, the researcher can plead ignorance.) As far as we have been able to tell, this does not in any way detract from the effectiveness of the technique; and incidentally, it is also cheaper.

3.2. *The semi-press release*

By this rather clumsy term, we mean 'press releases' which are half-way to being advertisements. A good example is the 'Buy Line', where we borrow the style and format of those features which appear in *Reader's Digest* and certain of the popular women's magazines, in which a variety of products are written up in a chatty, informal style, each one being allotted a brief paragraph and a simple line-drawing illustration.

We have found this kind of stimulus particularly useful when we want to evaluate some early thoughts on pack design as part of a concept. For example, in Plate 2 there is a 'Buy Line' we produced as part of a project for a paper manufacturer. (Our fake example is indicated by an arrow; the others around it are genuine.) This company had the technology for producing moist tissues and packaging them in boxes or other containers, to be pulled out one at a time as needed. Hitherto, such products had largely been available only in individual foil sachets; but, given a reasonably air-tight closure, the new version could be packed up to hundred or so in a container, and would stay moist to the last tissue. This, as one would expect, cut the cost per tissue to the consumer quite dramatically.

Our task was to explore possible applications for such tissues: with what liquids might they be impregnated, what could they then be used for, how might they be packaged and branded, and so on. We considered a host of ideas, from the obvious to the slightly wild; this was one of the wilder ones. Throwaway cloths (J-Cloths and similar brands) were just starting to appear on the market, and proving quite successful. Was there, we wondered, a place for a throwaway dishcloth, ready-impregnated with washing-up liquid – thus offering two products in one? Obviously, we were not – despite the claim in our copy – really expecting to replace washing-up liquid, but just a small share of that huge market would have been well worth having. And so the pack design, we felt, should be a little reminiscent of a washing-up liquid container – the tissues would be packed inside in a spiral, to be pulled out one at a time from the middle of the roll. Hence the simple illustration.

As it happened, the idea was not a success; people found the idea of using a separate tissue for each load of washing-up far too extravagant. But one small element in our concept *did* arouse interest: the idea of a tissue impregnated with germ-kill or disinfectant properties. Not for washing-up, perhaps, but for other applications altogether – a hint which sent us off on a whole new line of development. Once again, our press release had more than repaid its small cost; it had helped us rule out a blind alley, and suggested several new ideas to be followed up.

3.3. Press advertisements

Mocked-up 'press ads' for use as stimuli in research – the idea might seem far too obvious, and too self-explanatory, to be worth wasting many words on. Yet mock press ads, like the real thing, can come in a whole variety of guises; within this technique there are a good many finer points to be explored – in particular, the art of suiting the stimulus to the need. Just how elaborate does the ad have to be? Do we need illustrations – and if so, how many and of what kind? Must we have colour, or would black-and-white do as well? How crucial is the pack design – can we leave it out altogether at this stage, or conversely, should it dominate the whole ad? And so on.

The basic principle in all this – as we said earlier – should be 'Good enough to look convincing – and no better.' At this stage of the game, high gloss finish for the sake of it is sheer waste of money.

A mock press ad can be very simple indeed. Consider the next example (Plate 3) – scarcely more, in fact, than a glorified press release. Yet it proved quite good enough for its purpose.

The company in this case was Cow & Gate, the baby-food division of Unigate (already briefly referred to in Chapter 3). For years they had been producing milk-based foods for babies, and got themselves an excellent name for doing so. But now, they had a problem: in simple terms, too much milk and not enough babies. The birth rate was falling; there was a trend back to breast-feeding; and Cow & Gate found themselves with quantities of highly sophisticated milk-processing plant in danger of standing wastefully idle. They obviously needed to diversify into other activities, or other markets – but which?

We came to the conclusion that Cow & Gate could best diversify in two possible ways, by no means mutually exclusive. They could diversify *vertically*, drawing on their existing manufacturing capabilities – in this case, the processing of milk in powder form, for which they possessed expertise and machine capacity in a high degree. In other words, they could concentrate on doing other things to milk, and feeding it to other mouths than those of babes and sucklings. Or they could diversify *horizontally*, using the strength of their reputable brand-name, and provide for other needs of babies than the filling of their stomachs – such as nappies, or toys, or baby-clothes.

Both these approaches seemed promising – bearing always in mind that we must rule out any activity that might in any way weaken the Cow & Gate name, whose trusted place in the eyes of mothers was one of the company's greatest assets.

This ad represents some of our earliest work on the 'vertical' possibilities, when we asked ourselves: 'Who else could benefit from foods based on milk protein?'

One answer presented itself immediately. The dietary needs of old people are, in many ways, very similar to those of babies. Both need a high level of protein in a relatively small volume of food; babies because their sheer size precludes them from eating in bulk, and old people because their appetites, very often, are not what they were. Every doctor and social worker is all too familiar with cases of old people (especially those living alone) found dead, or taken into hospital, as a result of malnutrition – typically, it turns out that they have been living on bread and jam and cups of tea. The reasons they give speak of loneliness and apathy; they 'don't seem to have much appetite, these days', or 'it doesn't seem .worth cooking, just for me'. Or, of course, 'food's so expensive, nowadays'.

For old people like those, a milk-based protein food was ideal. It would provide a high level of nutrition in an easily assimilated, highly digestible form; only a very small quantity could supply most of their daily protein requirements. And it would not have to cost very much.

But – the crucial problem – could they be persuaded to take it? We had to find a way of explaining to them why they needed such a product, but without insulting them. After all, we none of us like to be told that we are getting old and doddering (even less so if it is at all true), that we cannot eat 'proper' food any more, that all we can manage is slops and babies' pap. Nobody – and who can blame them – is going to take kindly to being labelled 'geriatric' – and terms like 'old person', 'pensioner', or 'senior citizen' are not much better. So we were trying to find a way of putting across our message which would prove acceptable to our target market. This press ad is one of our earliest attempts; and, as it turned out, it was very close to the mark.

The stark simplicity of the layout was right, we felt, for the semi-medicinal area in which we were operating; so was the low-key, explanatory tone of the copy. At this stage, pack format was not crucial, so we had no need for pack design; but we did want to explore brand-name possibilities, and check on price expectations and possible flavours.

We put our 'ad' into research, with most encouraging results. Our approach proved to be highly acceptable; its tone was appreciated, and its message was understood. Even those respondents who still enjoyed hearty appetites readily accepted that they were unusually lucky, and admitted that even they had off days, when a product like Vital would come in useful. A few details were not quite right. The flavours were thought too sickly, too much like children's drinks (although variety as such was very welcome); why not more savoury flavours? This was a useful pointer for future development. Otherwise, only a minor point in the copy aroused criticism – not everyone understood, or liked, the word 'ingest'.

Once again, we had been able to gain a lot of useful information from one simple, very economical stimulus.

The next ad (Plate 4) may look a good deal more elaborate; but in fact it cost scarcely more to produce than the previous example. In this case, the company concerned had already chosen a field for diversification; they wanted to get into the wine market, which had been expanding steadily in the erstwhile non-wine-drinking countries of north-western Europe. As an international company, they were in a position to draw their supplies from any suitable source; but wanted to come into the market with a distinct point of difference. One possibility, we suggested, might be to avoid the traditional wine-lands of France,

Germany, Italy and Spain, whose products were crowding a highly competitive market; instead, why not choose one of the lesser-known countries, and set about improving and building upon its image?

Greece seemed an ideal choice. It produced large quantities of wine — much of which, we discovered, was currently being blended and sold as the produce of other countries, or of nowhere in particular. It had a long history of wine-making, far longer indeed than that of France. Its wines were of many sorts, often enjoyable, sometimes excellent — and always gratifyingly cheap. Our range would be a selection of the finest varieties.

Hence the ad. When illustrations are needed for mock press ads (either to help elucidate the concept, or simply because the ad would look wrong without them), we rarely find it worth going to the expense of photography. In this case, a travel brochure provided the pictures we needed; magazines are also a fruitful source, not least for the (real) advertisements in them; for food concepts, recipe books are invaluable. (Such piracy, of course, has to be kept strictly within research usage, for obvious reasons.) Our Greek wine ad was in colour; but it could equally well have been in black-and-white, had it been appropriate for the market.

Response was enthusiastic. Those who had not tried Greek wines were now eager to do so; those who had were prompted to nostalgic mutterings about little *tavernas* on the harbour-front. Overall, the image of Greek wine was much enhanced.

For certain kinds of product, pack design is an intrinsic element, and one that it is crucial to get right. This may be because the product will be incomprehensible to consumers unless they know what the pack looks like; or because, in some product fields, the pack virtually *is* the product. With cigarettes, for example, the pack is frequently all-important, the advertising image scarcely less so — the actual sticks of tobacco inside the packet are of little more than marginal significance in the mix. The same is true, to a lesser degree, of certain drinks, such as whisky, and vodka, and many cosmetics and perfumes.

Pack design therefore featured strongly in the next ad (Plate 5), part of a project for one of the big international tobacco companies. We were looking for an approach which would attract young people, a 'casual' brand (as against the rather more formal 'prestige' approach of such brands as Dunhill and Benson & Hedges). Our brand should have a touch of the American about it, without being totally transatlantic; and it should give the impression of having been around, in a quiet way, for quite some time.

In this ad (which was only one of several we tested) we went to a greater degree of detail and finish in the pack design than we would normally think necessary. The illustration, though, was once again 'borrowed' – in fact from a drink ad in a Dutch magazine. But it expressed well enough the concept we wanted to convey.

Of all the concepts we tested, Lancaster did best. Smoking, it seems, is still seen as a sociable activity – though non-smokers might well disagree.

Occasionally, we have found it worthwhile to take original photography for our stimuli – so long as it can be kept simple. In the next example (Plate 6), we wanted to illustrate a Jeeves-like butler presenting (with suitable hauteur) a helping of sausages on a silver salver; but nobody had been obliging enough to take the necessary photograph for us. True, we could have hired a model, and posed him suitably; but that would have been expensive. We decided we could achieve the desired affect by simply photographing the salver – a quick and inexpensive operation – and letting the copy supply the tongue-in-cheek element we wanted. The concept proved quite popular in research, but among too small a sector of the market to interest the manufacturer. A pity.

In another ad (Plate 7), we combined pack design with line drawing. Iglo, the Belgian frozen food company, wanted to find a way of introducing 'boil-in-the-bag' frozen products on to the Belgian market, where they were virtually unknown. (Frozen food is in any case far less developed in Belgium than in Britain or the

USA.) We suspected that the Belgians, a highly food-conscious race, might react strongly against the idea of prepared food 'in plastic bags', and therefore wanted a presentation which would make the whole idea seem less artificial and ultra-modern. Our solution was to make an analogy with an old-fashioned cooking method, 'bain-marie' (whereby one saucepan is placed inside another which is full of boiling water, to obtain a very steady cooking temperature). 'Boil-in-the-bag' thus became, not a dubious innovation, but simply an updated version of a reliable old method.

For our stimulus, we produced some rough packs, incorporating pictures from a recipe book, and combined them with a deliberately old-fashioned, stylised drawing, to demonstrate the product in action. The response was all we could have hoped for; our concept successfully overcame resistance to 'newfangled food products'. This range, with pack design based closely on our rough suggestions, and using the very same stylised drawing on the back, is now on the market in Belgium and (at the time of writing) easily brand leader in its market.

It is tempting to go on proliferating examples of mock press ads; but we feel we have shown enough to demonstrate what a versatile and flexible form of stimulus they can be; and how much 'presence' and realism can be given to a new product concept for a very moderate cost.

3.4. Posters and outdoor advertising

Consider Plates 8 and 9. A prime poster site, in the centre of Brussels, not a kilometre from the Grand' Place. In Plate 8 the site carries a poster for oranges, while in Plate 9, a new poster has been put up in its place, advertising Iglo.

It does seem a little odd, though, that the very same van is still parked directly underneath the poster − and that the driver apparently has not moved. Evidently a very patient man; or perhaps he is dead. ...

The answer, of course, is that the Iglo poster is a fake; it never existed. We took a photograph of the poster site; made an enlarged print from it; inserted into that print our own fake advertisement (using pictures borrowed from an advertisement for cookers); and then rephotographed the whole thing. The result: a fake poster on a perfectly real site.

For apparent 'realism', this technique is almost unbeatable, since it is still widely believed that the camera cannot lie. And it is ideal when one wants to test a broad, bold concept which can be briefly stated – the very kind of statement which appears on 'real' posters, in fact.

In this case, our 'product' was the whole company, Iglo. We were searching for an 'umbrella' concept under which to include a whole range of new product ideas, many of which involved foreign or exotic recipes – a range of Italian pasta dishes, for example, or frozen Chinese foods. One possibility, we thought, was to present Iglo as an adventurous, pioneering company, which searched the world 'discovering' foreign foods, and brought them back for the delectation of the Belgian consumer. Hence 'Iglo the Discoverers', which could form a baseline at the bottom of every advertisement. But in order to make it comprehensible, we wanted a single statement encapsulating our concept; and therefore created this poster.

'Exotic appeal' was also the thought behind our next 'outdoor' stimulus (Plate 10), which we conjured up on the side of a No 3 bus going round Trafalgar Square. In the long hot summer of 1976, various American (or supposedly American) brands of ice-cream, such as Dayville's and Baskin-Robbins, were selling well in Britain; should Wall's follow suit? Perhaps, we thought – but could there be other approaches, which could convey high quality and exciting flavours no less than 'American'? Switzerland, for example; a country with a reputation for quality products, and an excellent dairy image, not to mention a suitably chilly climate. So we created Wall's Swiss Ices, and put them on a bus, to see if we were on the right route.

As it turned out, Swiss ice-cream was OK, but Italian was even better; and the solution we finally came up with for Wall's had something of all of these approaches.

3.5. Voice tracks

The voice track, or mock radio commercial, is one of our favourite techniques; and it is a great pity that it is the only one we cannot illustrate, short of including a cassette with each copy of this book. (However, we would prefer to stay on speaking terms with our publishers.)

Of all the stimuli we have mentioned in this chapter, the voice track is the quickest to produce. It can be written at ten o'clock in the morning; recorded at eleven o'clock; and put into research by lunchtime. Not even the simplest press release can be produced as fast as that.

A further advantage is that commercial radio, in Britain at any rate, is entirely local, which provides an unassailable explanation why your respondents will never have heard the commercial you are playing to them. 'Ah yes, I believe this one went out on Radio Birmingham...' – or whatever city you are *not* conducting the research in.

Voice tracks have their limitations. They cannot be used for any concept which requires complex explanations; nor where the pack design is a crucial factor. But they are ideal for many food products – new forms of confectionery, for example – and we have made successful use of them when researching ideas for drinks, and ice creams, and almost any products aimed predominantly at a young market.

Although virtually anybody can, in theory, record a voice track, we have always found it is best to use somebody with broadcasting experience – an actor, or a disc jockey. Recording is then much smoother and quicker, and the artist can usually oblige with a funny voice, or a regional accent, if required.

Stock special effects are the voice track equivalent of scrap art.

Any good sound studio has a library of pub noises, applause, seagulls, 'rhubarbing', and other useful 'noises off' which can add enormously to the effect of a voice track; as well as a wide selection of all kinds of music to help create whatever mood is wanted.

Voice tracks come cheaper in bulk, unlike most other stimuli. Given a sufficiently professional presenter, it is quite possible to record half a dozen voice tracks within an hour, at much the same cost as for a single one.

3.6. Video

The idea of a mock television commercial might sound extravagantly ambitious; but it need not be. Using modern video techniques, and a reasonably simple format, it is quite possible to make a thirty-second colour 'commercial' for not much over £200. This can be worthwhile when, for example, one is dealing with a product field in which almost all advertising takes place on TV – washing powders are an obvious example – or when a demonstration of the product in action is central to the concept.

The demonstration-type commercial, in fact, provides an ideal format, since it generally requires nothing more than a presenter, a product, and a single camera position (with perhaps a zoom or two), plus a pack-shot at the end. It is also a format which respondents will find familiar (albeit not particularly enthralling). As with mock radio commercials, regional variations can be invoked to explain why people have not seen it before. On one occasion, to explain away some slightly rough camera work, we attributed our 'commercial' to New Zealand, an excuse which our British respondents seemed to find quite convincing – but no doubt a gross and wholly unjustified libel on the skills of antipodean TV technicians.

4. The uses of creativity

To say that new product development requires creativity might seem to be a truism too obvious to need stating. But, as we have tried to show in this chapter, it is not only (or even mainly) in *having* new product ideas, that creativity is needed; it is also vital in the development of those ideas – the whole painstaking, step-by-step process of brand building.

But it is perhaps a different kind of creativity that is required at this latter stage. As we have suggested in a previous chapter, no particular skills are needed to produce new product ideas; everybody, as Edward de Bono often points out, is potentially creative, given a little encouragement. The creativity needed for successful brand building, though, is rather more specialised; it calls on the skills of the copywriter, pack designer, illustrator, photographer, and researcher – for research also has its creative aspects, as we point out in the next chapter.

This form of creativity is of course less spectacular – which may be why it tends to get overlooked. 'Idea' creativity has news appeal – Archimedes leaping from his bath shouting 'Eureka!', Newton being stunned by his apple, mad-eyed cartoon scientists with light-bulbs flashing above their heads – such figures we all know and love. The less instant version of creativity – steady, craftsmanlike, and methodical in approach – may lack glamour by comparison. But as we have shown, it certainly has its uses.

6   Flexible research

1. Uses and abuses of research

1.1. 'Don't ask me. I just shop here'

Even in Britain, where market research costs are relatively low, it is very easy to spend a vast amount on research – and waste most of it. There are many showy, expensive, time-taking research methods, designed to bring forth impressively-tabulated results in the form of statistics, scales and graphs – and concealed there, all too often, is one small nugget of information which could have been discovered by common sense plus an hour or two's creative thought.

In an earlier chapter (pp 66–8), we have already explained why, in our opinion, Gap Analysis – when applied to new product development – is one such wasteful technique. We will not reiterate the arguments here, beyond saying that the basic fault, we think, lies in the use of market research in trying to identify new product opportunities – in other words, expecting the consumer to produce your new product ideas for you.

Obviously, we are not saying that consumers *cannot* come up with perfectly viable ideas and suggestions for new products. They can, and they frequently do. On many occasions, when we have exposed a given concept to research, respondents have made comments on the lines of: 'Well, I don't think I'm very interested in something that does *that* – but if it did *this*, now ...', thus giving us the germ of a promising new idea. Equally, in probing consumers' dissatisfactions in this or that field, we have often elicited responses which went far beyond mere negative criticism of existing brands, and included creative suggestions for new products. And of course, consumers (since, after all, all of us are consumers) can quite well come out with spontaneous ideas; everyone has had conversations which went: 'You know, somebody really ought to make something that would ...'

Our contention is simply that one should not *expect* consumers to produce such ideas, nor that their ideas, when produced, will be usable – which is the basic assumption behind such techniques as Gap Analysis. Any usable ideas that do emerge will only have been obtained at considerable expense; and the truly original new concepts – those that involve some kind of creative or 'lateral' leap – will almost certainly never emerge from such research at all.

In other words, when it comes to generating a list of new product ideas, the human imagination is far quicker, far cheaper, and infinitely more wide-ranging than any research technique could ever be. Once such a list has been arrived at, it is *then* that market research is needed – small-scale, inexpensive, qualitative research to test out, modify and narrow down the concepts that creative thought has produced. In the body of this chapter, we would like to discuss the best way to organise this kind of research.

1.2. Oh well, back to the drawing board

The other area of new product development where research, we think, is often missed, is after the brand building stage – where the fully-clothed concept is ready for evaluation. The main danger here is lack of flexibility – and again, it is not that results will not be forthcoming, but that the same (or better) results could have been obtained faster, and more cheaply.

All too often, the concept, or concepts, that have emerged from the idea generation stage will be fed straight into a large, elaborate research programme lasting several weeks; at the end of which it may turn out that, for example, the pack design chosen has unfortunate associations for most respondents, and that the concept has therefore done badly. Either one then has to make the assumption that, given a better pack, the concept could have performed better (which may not necessarily be true), or the pack must be changed, and the whole research programme lumbered through once more. Unsatisfactory, either way.

Probably in an attempt to circumvent this kind of problem, it is sometimes the practice to conduct research in a way that might be described as 'concept fragmentation' – i.e. the brand-name is tested, the pack design is tested, the product attributes are tested, and so on, each one separately and in limbo. A satisfactory result having been reached in each area, the various elements are stuck together, and the whole construction is re-tested – at which point, as often as not, it fails dismally, to the consternation of one and all. (The classic example of this kind of misapplied research is the Ford Edsel, where each element was enthusiastically received, and the car itself flopped. Ironically, so few were sold that the car has now become something of a collector's item.)

In contrast to this last approach, we have always strongly believed in testing the whole concept – what is sometimes called in the jargon, the 'hypothesis totality'. Once again, it is a question of asking consumers to respond to something they can reasonably be expected to evaluate – and a pack design, in limbo, without brand-name, price, or other product attributes, is not – in this sense – a reasonable stimulus. So it is hardly surprising that consumers' views on such product fractions tend to be unreliable, at best.

It is possible, we maintain, to avoid the pitfalls of both these research approaches: to test a complete brand, but to do so in such a way that individual elements of the concepts can be altered or amended if necessary, within the framework of the research programme, so that the correct 'mix' can rapidly be arrived at. This can be achieved given a sufficiently integrated and flexible research technique — one that we have nicknamed 'creeping research'.

2. 'Creeping' research

2.1. Ringing the changes

In the previous chapter, we outlined a number of techniques for creating realistic stimuli for use in research, and emphasised throughout that (with the possible exception of video) they could all be produced within a very modest budget. This is not merely cost-saving for its own sake (though that is no bad thing), but a vital factor within our research approach. Because a stimulus which is cheap to produce is going to be even cheaper to alter.

Say that a new product concept is fed into a programme of — for example — six group discussions. By the end of the first two groups, it may appear that the brand-name was ill-chosen — respondents are having difficulty in pronouncing it. Assuming that the researcher is in sufficiently close touch with the creator of the concept, this finding can be rapidly communicated — together, perhaps, with suggestions as to how the name might be improved. Within two days — or even less, if the stimulus is a voice-track or a press release — the concept can have been re-christened, and be re-inserted into the research programme.

The same is true of each other element in the mix. Indeed, given a research programme lasting two or three weeks, it is quite conceivable that every single element in a new product concept — name, pack design, product attributes, price, recipe, pack size, positioning — might have been altered while the research was in progress. (Like the old puzzle of the boots which had been re-soled and then given new uppers, it would be a nice philosophical point whether, in fact, one could then refer to it as being in any way the 'same' concept.) But by the end of the research, one could assume, with a reasonable degree of certainty, that the brand has been 'optimised' – that all the elements within it were now harmoniously combined, so that no one aspect might damage the others – and that the brand itself 'worked' as a complete entity.

The system is open to certain objections. 'Pure' researchers criticise it on the grounds that one can only test like against like, that two rival concepts must have *everything* in common bar the one aspect to be evaluated, if the findings are to be valid. Thus, they contend, if you combine brand-name A with pack format P, and test it against brand-name B attached to pack format Q, you have muddled the research picture, and your finding will not be conclusive. What you must do is test pack format P under brand-name A, against pack format P under brand-name B; you must then go on to test pack format P with name A, against pack format Q, with name A; then ... and so on.

This argument is, theoretically, quite true. But, given that most concepts have at least half-a-dozen attributes which can be isolated, it is obvious that the number of different permutations to be tested could rapidly become unmanageable. In reality – where most of us, for better or worse, have to operate – we think it is far better to construct an intelligent hypothesis (which is a polite phrase for an informed guess) on the lines of: 'According to all we know, a brand called *this*, packaged like *that*, positioned and priced *so*, seems likely to succeed – let's test it.' And if one factor or another proves wrong, it can be changed. The process is *ad hoc*, and theoretically questionable; but on the evidence of our experience, it works.

2.2. Lines of communication

'Assuming,' we said in the last section, 'the researcher is in sufficiently close touch with the creator of the concept ...' It is an important assumption – one worth dwelling on for a page or so.

By this stage in the book, it must have become obvious that we regard successful new product development as being based on two essential skills — those of the researcher, and those of the creative person. And creative skills, as emphasised in the last chapter, are crucial not only in generating new product ideas, but in representing those ideas in the form of realistic stimuli.

If these two specialists are to interact to best effect, it is essential that there should be close communication between them. First, so that they can come to understand each other's skills, and methods of working. The researcher can gain insight into that famed mystery, 'the creative temperament', and realise the potential scope of creativity intelligently deployed; the creative person can learn the mechanics of research, and how best to angle the work he produces for the researcher to make effective use of it. (Producing creative work for research can be very different from producing it for 'real'; a copywriter, for example, will often think in terms of an 'attention-grabbing' headline, and ultra-brief copy, both of which for the researcher's purposes may well be unnecessary, or even possibly undesirable.)

Secondly, as implied above, it can render the whole research process far quicker, more flexible, and (we contend) far more effective, if the researcher can maintain close communication with the creative person throughout. The altering and improving of creative stimuli may then be a matter of a few hours, rather than (as is too often the case) of several days or even weeks.

Indeed, it is a remarkable fact that, in the normal run of new product development, the research and creative specialists may have virtually no direct communication whatsoever. Often enough, they are in different companies, an advertising agency being employed to produce work in its creative department, which is then handed over to a research company. But even when all the work is being handled under the same roof, as when an agency fields its own research department, contact is often at a minimum. Typically, there will be an initial grand meeting, which representatives of the two departments (plus several others) will attend. Then, the creative head goes away, and delegates the work to a creative team. They produce work, pass it to the account executive to get client approval. This done, the executive takes the work off to the research department, who research it. A few weeks later, a research report is produced, and discussed at another grand meeting, prior to presentation to client. ...

Not surprisingly, under these circumstances, the two most essential contributors to a successful new product development plan have only the vaguest idea of each other's requirements.

Hence our insistence on an 'integrated' research technique – one in which the creative and research members of the team fully understand each other's activities, and can be in touch at a moment's notice. In fact, they may even – revolutionary though the thought may seem – be the same person.

3. Specific research methods

3.1. Quantity vs quality

Detailed discussion of research techniques does not come within the scope of this book, since research is only one of the tools – albeit essential – used in new product development. All we aim to do at this stage is to list some of the main standard research techniques which we have found useful, with a brief outline of the advantages and drawbacks of each as a means of evaluating new product concepts. At the brand building stage, we almost invariably prefer qualitative research – involving a relatively small number of people in detailed, informal discussions – to quantitative research, which can provide the reassurance of sheer numbers, but tends to lack subtlety. Small-scale, qualitative research allows for 'fine-tuning' of the kind needed in new product development – finding out not just how many respondents like or dislike a concept, but exactly what it is that attracts or repels them, and (with luck) how it might best be improved. Its corresponding weakness, of course, is that one is, by the nature of the technique, dealing with small numbers of people, and that any decisions which result may be based on the (possibly unrepresentative) opinions of a dozen or so respondents. For this reason, it is essential that any findings which emerge from this stage are eventually subjected to larger-scale research (as described in the following chapter).

Even in the relatively early stages of brand building, though, quantitative methods can sometimes have a place; at the end of this section we cover one form in which we have found it especially useful.

3.2. Group discussions

These are just what they sound like. Typically, about eight or ten respondents are assembled together, in informal surroundings (often somebody's sitting-room), and encouraged, under the guidance of a trained researcher, to discuss whatever needs discussing. The researcher's job is to keep the discussion more or less on the topic in hand, make sure all the crucial points are covered, throw in provocative questions when needed, and generally keep the show on the road. The group may be asked to consider some specific concepts, or simply to express their general attitudes to a given product field – or of course both.

Given a good researcher to guide them, group discussions can be richly informative and revealing. The presence of others often lends moral support; and respondents in groups may become far more articulate, and far more critical, than they would be in one-to-one confrontation with a researcher. The sheer momentum generated in a good group discussion can be exhilarating; every researcher can recall groups where the respondents, still in full and enthusiastic flow, had to be almost forcibly ejected from the room to make way for the next group.

Often, a vigorous argument may develop between respondents – which can be highly instructive (and entertaining) for the researcher. One respondent may like the concept under discussion; another finds it wasteful or unnecessary. How does the first respondent defend the product, and with what arguments? How does the other try to refute them? Who wins? Sometimes, we deliberately stimulate such arguments by introducing two contrasted press releases into a group: one in favour of a concept, the other attacking it. Or one may line up regular users of a particular product category against non-users – a technique known as a 'confrontation group'.

The weakness of group discussions is – as so often – the mirror image of their strength. A group can be 'railroaded' by one or two strong characters within it, and coerced or browbeaten into expressing unanimous sentiments on which several of its members, if left quietly to themselves, might be a good deal less dogmatic. This often leads to the phenomenon which we have named Group Approved Sentiments (or GAS for short): piously expressed opinions or behaviour patterns which correspond to how the group members feel they should be seen to act, rather than to what they do in reality.

Both sexes are equally prone to expressing Group Approved Sentiments; but women are notably vulnerable when it is a question of being seen as the conventional image of 'a good mother' or 'a good housewife'. A revealing example of this occurred when we were conducting a group on the subject of 'disposables' (clingfilm, aluminium foil, plastic bags, etc). Right at the start of the group one lady announced that *of course* she always washed out and re-used plastic bags, in tones which left little doubt that anyone who did not was a thriftless slut; at which the rest of the group members agreed, to a woman, that yes, of course, so did they. Purely from purchasing data, as well as from other groups we had conducted, we knew that habitual re-using of plastic bags was rare in Britain (as against in the Netherlands, where it genuinely seems to be the norm); so either our group was startlingly atypical, or they were being less than frank. On balance, we suspected the latter.

In that case, luckily, we could detect that our group was

producing inaccurate findings. One cannot always count on knowing, unfortunately, though an experienced researcher can often detect when a group is being skewed in this way, and can then report accordingly.

3.3. Individual interviews

As we implied in the previous section, this technique, in broad terms, is weak where group discussions are strong, and strong where they are weak. The interview (which again usually takes place in informal surroundings, typically the respondent's home) is conducted with only the respondent and the interviewer present, and can last anything from fifteen minutes to a couple of hours, depending on what is needed. (For our purposes, we tend to favour the fifteen minute version.) The interviewer is provided with a list of questions to be covered, but should encourage the respondent to talk freely.

The main potential weakness of the technique is that the respondent, lacking any moral support from fellow consumers, may become shy and tongue-tied, and give unrevealing monosyllabic answers; or, even worse (as far as the research is concerned), give the answers he or she thinks the interviewer would like to hear. The corresponding advantage is that respondents cannot be dominated or influenced by other consumers' opinions, and may well, being assured of confidentiality, be far franker about their true attitudes and behaviour.

It is apparent that the success of this technique depends – even more than in group discussions – on the skill and personality of the researcher. The choice of interviewer thus becomes crucial. In many product fields, we have found that good results can sometimes be obtained by using interviewers of the opposite sex to the respondents; for example, if prepared food is under discussion, a housewife may more readily admit to a man that she is prepared to take short cuts in her cooking; equally, a sympathetic female interviewer, investigating male toiletries, may persuade a man to drop the stereotyped 'masculine' attitudes he might otherwise feel called upon to adopt. The principle does not always hold good, of course; to use a male interviewer to ask women about, say, sanitary protection would be inviting disaster.

3.4. In-home tests

It is sometimes desirable, or essential, for respondents to have experience of the product simultaneously with being exposed to the concept. Often this can be achieved by providing samples in the course of a group discussion or interview; but in some cases a longer exposure to the product is needed (as it would be, for example, for a new kind of washing powder). In these cases, the usual answer is a small-scale in-home test (or placement test, as it is also known); consumers are given a sample of the product to keep and use over a certain period, at the end of which their reactions are gathered.

This technique allows wide flexibility both in the research design, and in the use of concept material. Generally, consumers are shown the press ad, or whatever, and briefly interviewed on their reactions; they are then given the product for the stated period; after which the interviewer returns, finds out reactions to the product, and once again shows the concept material. In this way, before-use and after-use reactions to the concept can be compared.

Another option is to show respondents the concept material only *after* the in-home test, so that their reactions to the product will have been unprejudiced. In-home tests can also be interestingly combined with group discussions, as for example when half the members of the group have had a month in which to sample the product, and the other half come to it completely new.

At what point in new product development should the product itself (or initial prototypes) be introduced? Impossible to make a hard-and-fast rule, as so much depends on the particular circumstances. But in general, if the product is available, and lives up to (or almost up to) the concept, it is no bad thing to introduce it from the start. Otherwise, and especially where making even a few samples will be an expensive business, it is better sense to test out the concept first, before committing further funds. The only exception are those concepts which we refer to as 'Instant Hurrahs' – i.e. where the concept can only be a good thing, and all depends on the product living up to its promise. For example, say the concept was for a washing powder which incorporated a built-in fabric softener at no extra cost, it is a virtually foregone conclusion that consumer response must be: 'Well, that's great, but let's see if it's true.'

3.5. Hall tests

A hall test is something of a compromise between qualitative and quantitative research. A number of products and/or product concepts is exposed in a hall, or other large room, and respondents file past each in turn, rather after the manner of judges at a dog show. Usually, the respondents are then briefly interviewed on their reactions to each concept; under normal circumstances, it is possible to cover up to a hundred people in the course of a day.

A variant on this technique is the theatre test, where respondents are seated in rows (rather than promenading round by ones and twos), and concepts are projected on screens. In this version, respondents are generally asked to fill in questionnaires on the concepts they are shown, rather than being interviewed.

Methods like these have the advantages and drawbacks one would anticipate. They are useful when a large number of concepts (say ten or so) need to be screened rapidly, and so can help with the shortlisting process; they also provide the reassurance of greater numbers; but of course they are not designed to investigate the finer details of product evaluation.

3.6. Syndicated 'Omnibus' surveys

This is the only fully quantitative method of research that we normally use at the brand building stage; partly for the good reason that it is inexpensive enough to fit within this stage of the average new product development budget. Every week, the large opinion-poll companies (such as Gallup) question a thousand or so people, selected on a strictly random basis. The initial questions asked are often political, but for a few pounds each, one can have additional simple questions (of the 'yes/no/maybe' sort) added to the poll. One can even test out concept material, since questions can take the form: 'Please read this advertisement; would you be interested in buying the product?'

By leaving a question on the survey for a few weeks, a research sample of several thousand can rapidly be built up. The 'creeping research' technique can also be used here, since a concept can easily be modified between surveys, and fed in again the subsequent week; although the relatively crude nature of the questions does not allow for probing into details of product concepts, nor for finding out just *why* a particular concept is disliked.

Omnibus surveys are also useful for providing elementary market data, such as – for example – how many people ever eat curry, when, and where; all broken down by age, sex, class, and region. This kind of basic head-counting, besides its usefulness within product development, can provide much of the essential data when we come to the forecasting stage, as described in the next chapter.

4. Creeping research in action

4.1. Enter the Dragon

The British have a reputation for being insular. But when it comes to food, we are second only to the United States in the amount of foreign food we consume. (Indeed, it is arguable, since America is the great melting-pot of nations, that no food is really 'foreign' in the USA – merely a local speciality.) Certainly the rapid spread of foreign restaurants across the country is one of the most noticeable phenomena of recent years – and one which, in our opinion, has contributed enormously to the gastronomic standards of the nation.

Birds Eye, as the country's leading frozen food company, had watched the foreign food revolution with some interest; at what point, they wondered, was it worth their taking an active part? Eventually, judging that the time was ripe, they called us in to see how best they might launch a range of 'foreign foods'.

Our first thought was – do people think of 'foreign foods' as such? We invented a range called Round Table (all in circular packs) which included a curry, a paella, a pasta dish, a sweet-and-sour dish, and so forth – and put it into research.

Our conclusion was – no, people do not think in terms of 'foreign food' when they are deciding what to have for dinner. No one says to themselves 'Let's eat foreign tonight,' or 'Let's have something international.' They are far more likely to think within national cuisines – 'Let's eat Chinese,' or 'How about a curry?' We accordingly reported back to Birds Eye that they should think in terms of a national range – possibly, in time, of a series of national ranges. But just one, to begin with, and there was little doubt which it should be.

We already had data to show that Chinese food is by far the most widely eaten kind of foreign food in Britain. Few towns are without their Chinese restaurant, and many villages have one. In the North of England, long-established fish-and-chip shops were closing down every week, to re-open as Chinese take-aways ('Sweet and Sour Chips a Speciality'). We set about creating Birds Eye's Chinese range.

Our first three pieces of research were set up in parallel, since none of them needed to wait on the results of the others. We simultaneously organised: (i) a head-counting exercise, on an Omnibus survey, to find out the size of our potential market and the most popular Chinese dishes; (ii) an attitude study, to find out why people went to Chinese restaurants, and what they liked about 'eating Chinese'; (iii) in the same group discussions, we fed in two press releases, describing four fictional Chinese food ranges about to hit the market – one offered complete meals, one consisted of separate dishes in one-person servings, and so on – to see which would be preferred.

We discovered: (i) that about thirty per cent of the populace ate Chinese food fairly regularly, either in a Chinese restaurant or buying from a take-away (almost nobody prepared their own Chinese food from scratch). These, we decided, must be our target market; few people were likely to be converted to Chinese food by a frozen range. (ii) That the key to the 'Chinese restaurant experience' was the sharing – the fun of ordering several dishes, and each person taking some from each. People also seemed to appreciate the 'suggested meals' section of a Chinese menu – even though they did not necessarily follow its advice. (iii) That – as was therefore to be expected – the 'new range' which offered single products, each in one-person servings, was by far the most popular.

We had made good progress. We now knew that our range must aim at allowing consumers to replicate the 'Chinese restaurant experience' in their own home. We knew which dishes should be included – our Omnibus survey had given us a clear list of the favourites. We knew that these dishes should come in single-person servings. We knew – crucial point – that the potential market was big enough to interest Birds Eye, who have strict minimum tonnage requirements for all their products. We knew approximate price levels – roughly in line with those of a good-quality Chinese take-away. All we needed now was a brand.

Our range, we decided, should have a name. This was contrary to Birds Eye's usual practice; hitherto, all their products had been described on the lines of: 'Birds Eye – Sliced Beef in Gravy' or 'Birds Eye – Pineapple Cheesecake'. We felt, though, that 'Birds Eye –

Sweet and Sour Pork' might sound unauthentic. At the same time, we certainly wanted to retain the Birds Eye branding, which would lend reassurance on product quality and hygiene. A range name, with suitably Chinese associations, seemed to be the solution; after considering various alternatives, we settled on Green Dragon.

Next, we set about creating some pack designs. Since the combining of different dishes was central to our concept, we wanted the range to stand out *as* a range in the shops; so we made the packs green. This fitted the brand name; it also made the packs conspicuous, as few other frozen foods used green packs. (There was a long-standing belief that green, in connection with frozen food, would suggest the product was 'off'. We thought this a little far-fetched.) There should be a dragon on the pack, of a Chinese, but friendly, description, an illustration of the dish (borrowed from a cookery book), the Birds Eye logo, fairly small, and the words Green Dragon, plus the name of the dish, both rather larger. On the back of the pack, we wanted to put a simplified version of a 'suggested meals' grid, to help people in combining the products together according to how many would be present at the meal.

The advertising positioning, we felt, should continue to reflect the same balance between authenticity and reassurance as on the pack. Our recipes should be the work of a genuine Chinese chef, but working in Birds Eye's employ at their kitchens. For research purposes, we accordingly created such a gentleman, whom we named Mr Wang Fu, and wrote an ad around him, in which he explained the excellence of the dishes he had created. We also gave him a few words to say on the back of the pack.

We were now ready to test our whole concept, in the form of a press ad in which the pack design featured prominently.

The results were very encouraging. The idea of the range was well-received, as were the suggested items in it. The pack design, the range name, and the dragon himself, were liked; the idea of buying several dishes, and making up one's own Chinese feast at home, met with great enthusiasm. Prices raised the usual grumbles, but were generally accepted. The only major criticism concerned Mr Wang Fu – not his function as creator of the recipes, but that he had been allowed to take over so much of the ad – and therefore could not be real. 'Birds Eye would never let some Chinaman write their adverts for them,' was a typical comment.

One other change was needed. We had a trade mark search carried out on the name Green Dragon, and found that it had already been registered by another company. Since, though registered, it was not currently in use, Birds Eye could quite possibly have bought it; but we felt that the exact name was not fundamental to the concept, and that something similar would do just as well. 'China Dragon', for example.

So we re-wrote our ad, reducing Mr Wang Fu to a more subordinate role, and using China Dragon as our range name. Back into research; results were as good as, or even better than, before. We therefore reported back to Birds Eye that the prospects looked highly favourable, and recommending that they should engage a reputable Chinese chef, and set him to create some recipes, with all possible speed.

Within a year, the Birds Eye China Dragon range was in test market. A few months later, the brand was selling nationally, and was worth five million pounds a year.

4.2. Trial by error

Creeping research – to put it at its most negative – could be described as a process of constructive mistake-making; since our mistakes, it is well known, are what we learn by. Or perhaps constructive guess-work would be a better term, since by no means every guess, after all, turns out to be a mistake. But if we *are* going to learn by mistakes, it is as well to ensure that we make them in the most auspicious manner – in such a way that we learn as much, and lose as little, from them as we can.

Hence the creeping research process: guessing, constructing

hypotheses in the light of what we know or can surmise, checking out our hypotheses rapidly and cheaply, moving in the light of the results a few steps nearer the best solution, making a few more guesses, ruling out blind alleys ... all at a stage of the game when such activity costs very little, and can tell us a lot. If mistakes are to be made, it is always best to make them early.

But that is looking on the most negative side. Viewed positively, the techniques we have described in this chapter could be summed up as research used creatively, imaginatively, and as flexibly as possible, to check out the maximum range of concepts in the minimum time, and to give the finally chosen concept the best possible chance of success.

One final hurdle remains in the development process − and forms the subject of our next chapter.

7   Forecasting

1. Product + concept testing

So far, this book has shown how a new brand is developed from the first identification of an opportunity, through the brand building stage, up to a precisely defined and visualised brand. We have shown how the optimisation procedure – the test-and-retest system we have called creeping research – makes extensive use of qualitative research.

We are now at a point where larger, quantitative research is required. This sort of test is variously called a 'marketing mix test', a 'total offer test' or a 'concept plus product' test. It need not be complicated. But as a minimum, it should:

(a) Have a sample size of at least one hundred members of the target market.

(b) Present these consumers with some form of concept material – again following the principles of 'realism' outlined in Chapter 5.

(c) Obtain some estimate of likely trial – based upon the concept material.

(d) Allow the respondents to use the product. In nearly all fields this should involve in-home use, over a period of days or weeks. Where preparation is relevant – as in a food product to be cooked – this is a common-sense precaution. But even where no preparation is required, it is still vital that the test takes place in normal circumstances. There is ample evidence that sips and nibbles can be misleading – especially if they take place when the respondent is not in the right mood. (For instance, who wants to eat a bar of chocolate straight after breakfast, or a bowl of hot soup on a blazing hot day? Yet hall tests – the most common form of product testing – can entail both these absurdities.)

(e) Obtain a measure of likelihood to buy, following product trial – together with any other diagnostic information (such as specific likes and dislikes of the product) which may be considered relevant.

1.1. Misuse of norms

If the results of this test look good, the company should be prepared to put the brand (at least) on test market. If they look bad, then it is back to the drawing board. The only trouble is that the company may be unable to say what is a good result and what is a bad one. Often the results are assessed against norms; but as these norms are no more than averages of a haphazard series of previous tests, ranged over a number of probably disparate product fields, they are difficult to interpret. Possibly the company can tell from the norms whether it is likely to have a tremendous success on its hands, or an outright failure; but with anything in between the company can only cross its fingers and hope for the best, apart from putting right any small points of criticism to emerge in the course of the test. (There is, incidentally, a fallacy in the use of norms, if the criterion of success is defined as 'beat the norm'. Norms are averages, and averages summarise results that are both better *and* worse than the average. Every result that beats the average therefore increases the average; if the company has a run of successes the norm will get higher and higher; and it will be increasingly difficult to beat.)

Recently we saw a product test in which ten per cent of the sample said that they would definitely buy the brand. The research company, comparing with a norm of twenty per cent, ruled that the product could not possibly succeed. Yet the product field was one where a regular purchaser would need to buy about twelve packs a year; and even five per cent of consumers buying at this rate would have provided a highly profitable market for the company.

1.2. To launch or not

In this chapter, we show how test results can be meaningfully applied in the context of a simple forecasting system. The key question is not 'Have we beaten the norm?', but 'Do these results offer us the chance of a profitable market?' And this is a question which is peculiar to the circumstances of a particular company in the context of a particular market. For example, Unilever and Johnson Wax (if we could ever imagine them both in possession of the same test data) might reach opposite conclusions on whether or not to launch a particular new product – and both could be right.

2. 'But forecasting is impossible, isn't it?'

Anyone who *can* forecast the future accurately is able to reduce his risks. It is not surprising, therefore, that divination has been a preoccupation of man since history began. Few people question the *need* to know the future; only the *means* of forecasting it. Roman generals who peered at the entrails of disembowelled chickens are not nowadays criticised for wishing to know the outcome of their forthcoming battle; only for assuming that guts are very revealing. Similarly today, weathermen are not cursed for trying to tell us what tomorrow's weather will be; only for getting it wrong.

Any businessman engaged in launching a new product needs no convincing that a forecast of his likely sales would be invaluable. But he does need convincing that there is a forecasting method which has a predictably high rate of accuracy. The purpose of this chapter, therefore, is not to convince readers of the desirability of forecasting, but of how an accurate system may be constructed.

2.1. Use of backroom boys

At this point, the desire to call in an expert is very strong. Roman generals used priests; modern marketing men use statisticians, computer programmers, and market researchers. Nor are we necessarily denigrating this approach; except for the danger that the expert may not be sufficiently versed in the market, or the company, to produce a valid forecast; and the danger that the forecast will be cloaked in technical language that the marketing man will not understand.

We believe in a system that is understandable to the marketing man, and operable by him – a kind of do-it-yourself system, in fact. Because it is operable by the man who has to take the decisions, he is more likely to use it properly, and understand its shortcomings. If he knows what assumptions he has had to make, he will know what reliability to place on his answers.

2.2. No system guarantees certainty

No forecasting system is guaranteed. Inputs which rely on market research are subject to sampling error – that is, the 'true' result will lie in a range several percentage points either side of the sample result; and even this is only probably, rather than certainly, true. (The usual degree of certainty put on research results, for the purpose of calculating sampling error, is ninety-five per cent.)

The world can change: a political poll taken in the UK shows that the Labour Party, say, would win a majority of the votes cast, but six weeks later, the actual election result may be different. A brand launched in lone splendour may do extremely well – until a large competitor comes along. In this way, Heinz was able to disrupt the business of Nutriplan and Limmits, when it launched its range of low calorie soups against their meal-replacement soups.

But a system should be able to offer good odds of success. As any gambler knows, if he can obtain favourable odds for his bets, he will, in the long run, make money. Casinos, too, know this, which is why they offer the punters unfavourable odds.

Experience with our forecasting system leads us to believe that it will come up with the right answer (what we mean by the right answer we will come to in a minute) between seven and eight times out of ten. That may not sound very good; but it is a lot better than the historic rate in the marketplace, where, as we have mentioned earlier, up to eighty per cent of new products fail.

3. Profit from favourable odds

We observed in Chapter 3 that eighty per cent of new products fail, which means that for every five products launched by a manufacturer only one, on average, will make him money. Thus, if he accepts that launching new products is like gambling against odds of 4 to 1, he would be sensible to attempt new product ventures only if he could be sure that, whichever of his five succeeded, the profits would cover the losses of the other four. On the other hand, if he could shorten those odds to 3 to 2 on (three 'hits' for every two 'misses'), he would be in a much stronger position. An analysis of new product profitability by rate of success (Figure 7.1) shows clearly the dramatic effect of shortening the odds.

Firms A and B each launch five new products at an annual production cost of £1.0 million per product. Successful products, for the sake of the demonstration, gross £1.2 million annually whilst failures return only £0.5 million. Both companies kill failures after one year. Firm A achieves one success out of its five (the

Table 7.1   New product profitability – by rate of success

		Firm A	Firm B
Year 1	Number of new products		
	launched	5	5
	Cost per product	£1.0m	£1.0m
	Total launch year cost	£5.0m	£5.0m
	Number of successful products	1	3
	Return on successful products	£1.2m	£3.6m
	Return on unsuccessful products	£2.0m	£1.0m
	Total return on year	£3.2m	£4.6m
	Net profit on new products	– £1.8m	– £0.4m

		Firm A	Firm B
Year 2	Number of products continued	1	3
	Cost of running	£1.0m	£3.0m
	Return	£1.2m	£3.6m
	Net profit	£0.2m	£0.6m
	Accumulated profit over both years	– £1.6m	£0.2m

		Firm A	Firm B
Year 3	Number of products continued	1	3
	Net profit	£0.2m	£0.6m
	Accumulated profit over 3 years	– £1.4m	£0.8m

		Firm A	Firm B
Year 10	Number of products continued	1	3
	Accumulated profit over ten years	–	£5.0m

'typical' rate); Firm B, who believes in systematic new product development and forecasting, achieves three successes. After ten years Firm A finally breaks even on its original investment – no account taken of rate of interest on debt or inflation – whilst Firm B went into surplus on its new product account by the end of year 2, and shows a £5 million profit after ten years. Even if Firm A were able to squeeze a bigger return on its failures – £800 000 instead of £500 000 – it would take four years to reach break-even.

Clearly, it is financial lunacy to treat new products as a lottery with odds of 4 to 1 against. Yet that would appear to be the odds which most companies accept, albeit tacitly.

At the same time, no manufacturer – or forecaster – can guarantee success. Even the best laid plans can come unstuck; a forecaster can do no better than shorten the odds – not remove them. But dramatic shortening of odds – even though nothing like certainty is guaranteed – can turn new product investment into a profitable activity. After all, Firm B made £5 million in ten years – even though two of its products failed.

4. Forecasting instead of test marketing

There is a school of thought which insists that no amount of pre-launch planning or testing can determine whether success or failure is likely. The final go/no-go decision is left to the results of a test market. The thinking goes something like this: first, we will do everything we can to optimise all aspects of the product; then we will test market it; and on the basis of the test market, we will decide either to roll the brand out nationally or to kill it.

The only trouble with this procedure is that it is too drastic; to fail in test market is an expensive kind of failure, even though it is a lot cheaper than failing nationally. Ideally, companies would like a system which could tell them, with reasonable reliability, whether or not to launch, long before incurring the heavy investment needed for a test market.

Test markets have the following disadvantages:

(a) They do not provide much diagnostic data; considerable research is required to understand whether the brand is suffering from poor distribution, poor awareness, poor trial, or poor repeat buying. This tends to mean that test markets are little better than dress rehearsals for national launch – to ensure that all the various cogs in the production and sales process are operating smoothly in readiness for the national roll-out.

(b) The trade do not like them very much, which means that it is difficult to buy the same level of distribution that is possible nationally.

(c) The competition are alerted to the company's intentions, which often gives them time to prepare for the national event, and may even allow them to sink the test market by exceptional media or promotional activity. Unheralded national launches are much more difficult, and expensive, to counter successfully.

Our forecasting system is designed to answer all the questions that a test market ought to. First, and foremost, should the brand be launched at all? We know of a marketing company which used broadly our system alongside a number of its test market launches. It was found that, seven times out of ten, the forecast gave the same answers as the test market – i.e. 'launch' or 'don't launch'.

We do not claim our forecasting system to be a perfect predictor of actual sales right down to the last case; but it *is* good at saying whether the brand is worth launching or not. This means:

(a) The manufacturer now has the opportunity to launch nationally (or at least into several areas at once) with less risk of alerting the competition.

(b) A verdict can be reached much faster than by a test market. It may take a year at least to read a test market; a forecasting programme can be completed in under six weeks.

(c) The research of concept and product (which is necessary to provide the inputs for the forecasting 'model') provides at the same time a means of answering any diagnostic issues still unanswered by the smaller-scale 'creeping' research. For example, some aspects of product content (like level of sweetness) or positioning (such as whether the product can be made with cold as well as hot milk) can be resolved at this stage.

5. A new product purchasing model

Figure 7.1 is our 'model' of how a new brand comes to be purchased. It works like this:

5.1. Target market

For any brand there is a target market – be it housewives, heavy coffee buyers, automatic washing machine owners, or smokers who smoke king-size cigarettes only at weekends. To make the model work, we need to know the numerical size of that target market. Although defining a target market is not absolutely cut and dried, we can see that in principle the task cannot be overwhelmingly difficult. It is advisable to stick to the most important buying groups, since these are generally the easiest to define tightly, and the most sensitive to new brand testing (see page 160). For example, if ninety-five per cent of the sales of a product are bought by housewives with automatic washing machines, there is little point in considering non-owners of automatics, since their contribution is insignificant.

As a general rule, our model errs on the side of pessimism, since this is safer. Each approximation takes the worst view of what could happen. Hence we ignore minor parts of the target market.

5.2. Media weight

The first task of a new brand is to inform the target market of its presence. If people do not know a brand exists, they are hardly likely to buy it, except by accident; and few brands can survive on their accidental sales. Awareness generally comes in one of four ways: from media advertising; from promotional material (such as coupons through the door); from shelf facings or other in-store display; and by word of mouth. For fast-turnover packaged brands it is our experience that advertising expenditure has the greatest effect. (Anyway, it is difficult to isolate the other effects precisely, since they are so closely tied into media activity – promotions are advertised, shelf facings are easier to get when media spending is promised, and so on.)

5.3. Awareness

Media weight builds up awareness amongst the target market. For the purpose of the model, we assume that anyone not aware of the brand fails to buy it – again a deliberately pessimistic assumption.

5.4. Advertising effectiveness

Awareness is only the first hurdle which a new brand has to overcome. Being aware of a brand is not the same as buying it. The percentage of those made aware of the brand who subsequently buy it will depend, first of all, on how persuasive the advertising is.

5.5. Would try

The more effective the advertising, the greater the proportion of consumers who will buy it; or rather who feel they would like to buy it. Whether they can actually buy it or not will depend on distribution.

5.6. Distribution

Few new products are so innovative that consumers will hunt high and low for them. Many years ago Wilkinson launched their stainless steel razor blades in very poor distribution; yet the product was such an improvement over competition that men

Figure 7.1 A new product purchasing model

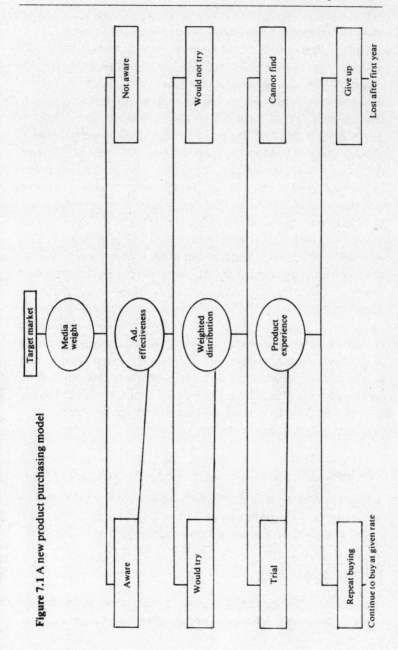

really would search for a chemist who stocked them. But this is the exception that proves the rule; most brands need widespread distribution to achieve sales. We take the view that if a brand has only a fifty per cent (weighted) distribution, then only fifty per cent of those who would like to buy the brand will in fact do so — because only half of them will be able to find it.

We believe that the logic of this conclusion is inescapable — though our assumption of a one-to-one relationship between distribution of a product and consumers' ability to find it needs justification. How can we be certain that twenty per cent distribution does not mean that thirty per cent of consumers will be able to find the brand? Or only ten per cent? Or, if a brand has ninety per cent distribution, surely that means that virtually everyone — i.e. one hundred per cent of the target market — will be able to find it? And could not there be differences between one market and another? Only a very large programme of experimentation — probably over many product fields lasting many years — will provide conclusive answers to these questions; in the meantime, we defend the assumption on the grounds that it is intuitively plausible, and that it seems to work. Also, it is a reasonably *safe* assumption — i.e. one which is unlikely to lead to gross error; whereas a bad mistake in the trial or repeat buying estimate can lead to a forecast which is wrong by several hundred per cent.

5.7. Trial

A target consumer who passes all these hurdles — who has been made aware of the brand, wants to buy it and finds it on the shelf — is able, at last, to put money down and buy it.

5.8. Product experience

A lot of brands fail because the product experience did not live up to the expectation. Advertising people often say — particularly of failed cosmetics, perfumes or drinks – that the image was wrong; but in a lot of cases the real fault lay with the product. Trial was achieved, but one experience was enough. The first experience of the product is therefore crucial for a new brand, since this experience will determine whether the consumer rejects the brand, or goes on to buy it again.

5.9. Repeat buying

If the product experience was good the consumer will be prepared to buy again – will become a repeat buyer*. If the product experience was bad, the consumer will reject the brand totally. Since most new brands are heavily supported at launch, the lion's share of potential awareness will have been achieved in the first year. This means that in the second year of its life the new brand will be relying heavily, if not entirely, on its repeat buyers from the first year. Even if things do not work out quite like that – a brand might start small, do rather well and earn the chance for heavier promotion in its second year – it is as well to assume that our model is correct, although that again is a pessimistic assumption, rather than rely on lots of extra trial in the second year to carry the brand through. Once everyone who can try the brand has done so, sales must rely on repeat purchase. A satisfactory repeat purchase rate is therefore imperative.

6. Market research simulation

Section 5 described how a new product comes on to the market and is bought. The purpose of constructing this purchasing model

---

* This implies the (perhaps questionable) assumption that a consumer who buys the brand *twice* before deciding about it counts as a 'repeat buyer'. We would like more evidence on this point, though in our experience the model works well as it stands. Extensive repeat buying prior to rejection tends to occur, we have found, mainly in the case of ranges, where the consumer tries each item before dropping the brand as a whole – multiple trial, rather than trial and repeat.

is to simulate this process, using data from our product + concept tests. Here is the simulated version (Figure 7.2):

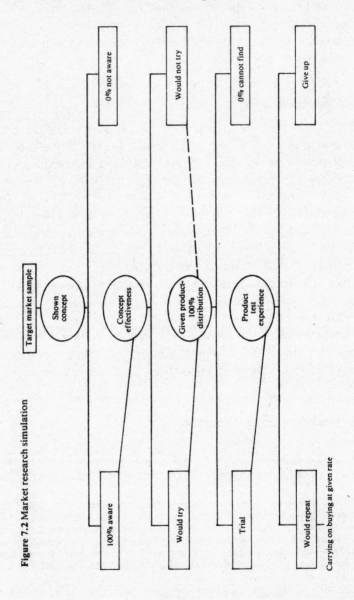

Figure 7.2 Market research simulation

6.1. Sample, not census

We draw a sample from the target market population rather than use everybody. Hence the need, outlined in 5.1, to have the target market tightly defined.

6.2. Maximum awareness

In research we show a concept advertisement – of the sort described in Chapter 5 – to our sample of the target market. The main difference between this procedure, and spending money on media space and time in the real world, is that we have a captive audience. *We create, by the nature of the test, one hundred per cent brand awareness.* In real life, awareness is nearly always less than one hundred per cent, even for really big brands. We believe that failure to take into account this difference is one of the most frequent errors which occurs in practice, when companies use market research results to arrive at sales estimates.

6.3. Likelihood to try

In our test we cannot ask our respondents actually to buy the brand; but we can ask them how *likely* they would be to buy it at a given price, if they could find it in the local shops. At this point, their knowledge of the brand is still based upon the concept advertisement. We allow them to answer in terms of a five point scale:

I would definitely buy it;
I would probably buy it;
I might or might not buy it;
I probably would not buy it;
I definitely would not buy it.

   Although we go to the trouble of having five points in our scale, and although an analysis of the distribution of answers can be extremely interesting – for example in distinguishing a 'love it or hate it' product from a 'quite like it' one — we ignore all but the first point of the scale (definitely buy) for the purposes of our forecast.*

We like this particular scale for three reasons: first, it is a question which respondents find relevant and easy to answer; secondly, it is a scale with a reasonable pedigree from the technical literature — being both predictive and discriminating; and thirdly, we have found that we have achieved prediction success with it ourselves in nearly forty cases. That is, we believe it is possible from this scale to derive the theoretical level of product trial that would result for a new brand — provided the brand could achieve one hundred per cent awareness (and one hundred per cent distribution — see next section).

6.4. Maximum distribution

In our test any respondent who says he will buy the brand after seeing the concept is given a product to try.** Thus the test now differs from real life in two respects: not only does it create one hundred per cent awareness, it also effectively creates one hundred per cent distribution.

In the market place, of course, very few new brands achieve anything like one hundred per cent distribution. And failure to take this difference into account is the second frequent error which occurs when people try to turn market research results into sales estimates.

6.5. Repeat purchase propensity

After the product has been tested, respondents are again asked their buying propensity, using the same five point scale. This

---

* We ignore all but the first point, because we find this gives as good a 'fit' with reality as putting buying probabilities against all the points on the scale.

** In all probability, we would also offer the product to those who said they would not buy it — hence the dotted line in Figure 7.2 — but that need not concern us for the forecasting model.

provides us with an estimate of repeat buying amongst trialists — i.e. how many will give up, and how many will carry on buying — at a given rate (see next section).

6.6. *Buying frequency*

The final piece of information we require to complete our forecast is an estimate of the likely frequency — in terms of number of packs per year — with which our repeat buyers will continue to buy the new brand. One method is to conduct further larger-scale research testing, such as the mini-test-market service operated by Research Bureau Ltd in the UK. This is a van selling operation where the product is offered for actual sale against competing brands, and its purchase frequency and total sales analysed over several months or a year. This method has been shown to be a very good predictor of buying frequency; its only snags are (i) the enormous cost of having to produce several thousand product samples, all in finished printed packs; (ii) the high cost of the research itself; and (iii) the long delay created between the stages of building the brand and launching it.

A simpler method is to conduct the normal product + concept test, but repeat it many times — offering respondents a choice of both the test brand and existing brands at every call. (A variant of this technique where respondents are given money and asked to spend it on a brand of their choice — from a list including the test brand — has been pioneered in the USA. Called CORE, it provides a measure of repeat purchase and buying frequency over a period of several months.) But these approaches, too, are costly and time-consuming.

In those cases where the new product is designed to create its own market, such as Homepride Cook-in Sauce — there may be no alternative to conducting some very elaborate research test of this type; no alternative, that is, except pure guesswork — or, even worse, relying on consumers' own future estimates as to how likely they will be to buy the new product — this being perhaps the most dangerous method of all.

Luckily, however, most new products are designed for markets which already exist, and where there are reasonably well-defined competitors. And luckily, too, it is reasonably easy to establish the buying frequency of the existing brands on the market. If the data is not published, it can be obtained from a consumer panel. (Most research companies operating a consumer panel, such as Attwoods, will be happy to sell the necessary data, without any commitment to become a regular subscriber to the panel.) Or it can be obtained from a simple survey where consumers are asked to say how recently they bought a particular brand. Although this method is less accurate that a consumer panel, it is certainly far more reliable than expecting consumers to predict their *future* buying patterns.

But how do we know that our new brand – if it succeeds in gaining awareness, distribution, initial trial and repeat purchase – will end up by being bought at the same rate as the brands currently on the market? Luckily again, we have a considerable body of evidence (see Andrew Ehrenberg's 'Laws of Marketing'*) which demonstrates that buying rates, amongst loyal users, tend to be equal for all brands in a market. Brand X may be more successful than brand Y, but the loyal users of brand Y will buy exactly the same number of packs in a year (even though there are fewer of them) as the loyal users of brand X. This is true unless (i) the pack sizes are different – in which case, not surprisingly, the rate of purchase is greater in inverse proportion to the size of the pack; or (ii) if one of the brands on the market happens to have many additional functions – and thus is really competing in more than one market at the same time. (An example of the latter is Dettol, which is used both as an antiseptic, where it competes with TCP; a disinfectant, where it competes with Jeyes; and even as a bath additive, where it indirectly competes with bath foams and oils.)

Our recommendation, therefore, in nearly all cases, is to arrive

---

* A.S.C. Ehrenberg, 'The Discovery and Use of Laws of Marketing', *Research*, Volume 9, Number 2.

at an estimate of buying frequency which is based upon an analysis of the buying frequencies of brands currently in the market, plus a large dose of common sense.

7. Right, let's get on with it

We are now in a position to make the forecast. The mathematics are simple. First, we take the number of consumers in the target market, in millions (let us call them M), and multiply by the trialists (t) expressed as a percentage of the target market. Then we must take into account the fact that not all trialists will become regular buyers, by multiplying again, this time by regular buyers as a percentage of trialists (let us call this figure r). Then our estimate of the number of packs per year (N) must be brought into the equation, and we multiply again. We now have a theoretical forecast: a forecast of the maximum potential for our new product, assuming we could create one hundred per cent awareness and one hundred per cent distribution. As we know we cannot, we must 'aim off', and multiply (thus reducing the estimate) first by the awareness level we hope to achieve (a), and then by the likely level of distribution (d), both expressed as percentages. For mathematical readers, the formula is therefore :

$$M \times t \times r \times N \times a \times d = \text{VOLUME SALES}$$

7.1. A complication

The extreme simplicity of the above formula is partly due to the fact that we have ignored once-only-trialists. This is deliberate. We have argued (Section 5.9.) that once-only trialists are virtually lost after the first year, and that it is very unwise to rely upon further trialists in Year 2. For most forward-planning purposes, or for comparing forecasts of different new products prior to drawing up future launch plans, once-only trialists are a complication best forgotten. But if the purpose of the forecast is to obtain the best possible estimate of the number of cases of a new product likely to be sold in the first year (as, for example, if a firm has to place a precise order with a co-packer, or a component supplier), then obviously once-only trialists must be added in. To do this, we simply take the target market in millions (M), and multiply by those trialists who do *not* become repeat buyers (i.e. t multiplied by 100 minus r*). Since they buy only one pack, there is no need to multiply by N; just by 1. Then they should be added into the forecast. The formula then becomes:

$$\text{VOLUME SALES IN FIRST YEAR} =$$
$$[M \times t \times r \times N \times a \times d] + [M \times t(100-r) \times a \times d]$$

7.2. An instant objection

At this point, the reader may object: 'But surely that means that the brand is bound to do worse in Year 2 than in Year 1? And there seems to be no way it can increase its sales in Years 3 and 4!' This, of course, is not the case: any of the inputs to the formula can change over time, and post-launch research can indicate where we need to revise our estimates upwards in the case of a successful brand, and downwards in the case of an unsuccessful one. But this is leading us into the field of sales forecasting for on-going brands, which is not what this chapter, and certainly not what this book, is about. Even so, it is worth noting how, in our experience, a successful brand continues to grow in its initial years: it normally does so *not* by increasing its acceptability amongst trialists, and certainly not by improving its rate of sale (in terms of number of packs per year) amongst its regular buyers, but quite simply by an increase in awareness and distribution – especially the latter – which produce a proportionate increase in sales, just as our formula would suggest. If therefore, the reader wishes to use the

---

* If r is the percentage of trialists who become repeat buyers, then 100 − r is the percentage who do not, and t(100 − r) is the percentage of the total target market who do not become repeat buyers.

formula to forecast sales of a new brand for several years ahead, he should make a set of estimates for awareness and distribution for Year 1, Year 2, Year 3, Year 4, etc – possibly exploring the effects of different build-up assumptions – and examine the alternative sales estimates which the forecasting formula gives him.

8. Estimating awareness and distribution

But how does a manufacturer estimate awareness and distribution for a new product in the first place – let alone for several years ahead? We have little advice to give except that past experience plus common sense should be used in abundance. Also, in our observation, manufacturers are quite good at estimating likely distribution levels, and, in conjunction with their advertising agencies, at estimating awareness. The usual procedure is something like this:

(a) Look at the existing brands on the market to see what the normal levels are. It would be unrealistic, for example, to opt for awareness or distribution levels greater than those of the brand leader.

(b) Look at a range of possible media budgets, and get an estimate from the agency of what are the best and worst awareness levels that these could buy; then take the average – or work the formula out using both.

(c) Look at past performance in winning distribution in this type of market with this type of outlet; again take a best and worst estimate.

9. Other uses for the model

The model is designed mainly for use at a final stage – instead of, or just prior to, a test market. But there is also a good case for using the system early on, when markets are being screened (see Chapter 3). We can put 'guesstimates' of trial and repeat purchase into the model, and see whether, on the basis of a reasonable guess, the market is worth considering further. Or the marketing man can put in his minimum tonnage requirement as the sales target, make reasonable assumptions about awareness and distribution, and then see whether the trial and repeat purchase rates which would be required are at all feasible. If it turns out that a market could be profitable only if every member of the target market bought the brand, then it is patently not worth considering further.

Used in these ways, our forecasting model provides a highly practical tool, perfectly geared to many aspects of systematic new product development, as well as a means of answering the final, $64 000 question – whether or not to launch.

8 New product guidelines – and some cautionary tales

1. Learning from experience

'All generalisations', it has been said, 'are dangerous – including this one.' And if there is one single lesson we have been able to draw from our experience in creating new products, it is that every case is different. (Which, if nothing else, certainly helps to make life interesting.) Nonetheless, we have tried in this book – perhaps at the risk of over-simplification – to outline some of the general principles behind our system of new product development, in the hope that the reader will be able to take our ideas and make good use of them, adapting and modifying them wherever necessary. (If, by this stage, it has not become clear that flexibility is a *sine qua non* of our system, then we have failed dismally in our intentions.)

In this final chapter, then, we would like to list a few extra points which either were not covered in the preceding chapters, or in our opinion deserve more thorough discussion than they have had so far. We would be reluctant to dignify these points with any term so grand as 'general principles' since (as we have said) we doubt whether there *are* such things in new product development; 'guidelines' might be a better term. In other words, these are thoughts to bear in mind in carrying out any kind of new product activity, and to be applied if and when appropriate.

Interspersed with these guidelines, and on occasion serving to illustrate them, are certain anecdotes which we have termed 'cautionary tales'. New product development is, as yet, a minefield – and largely uncharted. There are no Chairs in Diversification at even our most progressive universities; no Berlitz or Teach Yourself courses in product development; even books on the subject, such as this one, are at present very rare. Newcomers to the field (such as were the authors of this book, only a few years ago) have had little choice but to learn from their own mistakes.

Fortunately (for us, at any rate), other companies too have had their less successful moments. In the course of this chapter, we shall describe (with names and details omitted where necessary, to protect the innocent – and the guilty) various disasters and near-misses in the new product business over the last few years. Some of the incidents are drawn from our own experience, others we have heard of, and some have become part of marketing history. But we hope they will all prove entertaining – and instructive.

2. Know when to cut your losses

The trouble with a new product development programme, according to a senior marketing executive from Wilkinson Sword (reporting on the company's new product successes and failures in a Sunday newspaper), is that the new product idea may often acquire its own momentum, and become virtually unstoppable. Senior executives in the company become committed to the idea, a launch timetable is drawn up, enthusiasm reaches a peak; at this point there is a danger of a not-too-favourable research result being ignored. It is a brave market researcher who tries to stop a new product venture when the date of the sales conference is already fixed – especially if the research results are merely disappointing, rather than disastrous. If any decision is taken in the light of such last-minute warning signs, it will probably be a resolution to try even harder.

It would certainly be a pity if our insistence on a systematic approach to new product development – with its emphasis on a step-by-step programme – were to lead companies into this trap. At the very least, we should all be aware of the possible danger, and be able to recognise it. The danger is probably greatest at the point where the new project gets top management backing. First, a possible opportunity is spotted; then a middle-management team is appointed to explore the opportunity, perhaps with the help of external consultants. The team develops an idea to the brand building stage, and first results from small-scale research are encouraging. The time has come to present the case to the board. In the board meeting, the idea meets its first resistance, but after a spirited defence from the spokesman of the development team, the board vote funds for the project to be progressed to test market. The team therefore proceed to create a prototype product, which is put into a product + concept test; but a disappointing level of consumer interest is indicated. What should the team do now? Obviously the correct course is to report back to the board – even at the risk of encountering an 'I told you so' reaction. But the temptation to keep quiet about the research, or to write it off as misleading on technical grounds, will be very strong.

There are two points in our development programme where the decision to abort the project, and start again, could be a sensible course of action. These are: (i) after the brand building stage, if a large number of alternative positionings have been explored but no real spark of consumer interest aroused; and (ii) at the concept + product testing stage, if the levels of trial or repeat buying lead to a pessimistic forecast. If the results are sufficiently negative at either of these stages, the new product developer should have the courage of his convictions, even if it may mean some temporary discomfiture.

3. Understand the nature of a range

Throughout this book we have tended to refer to *the* new product, as if all new product development took the form of creating, developing and launching a single product. But just as often the new venture will consist of a *range* of products, such as a range of speciality teas, of frozen desserts, of car accessories, men's toiletries or holidays behind the Iron Curtain.

How does a systematic new product development programme cope with this complication?

3.1. Constructing a range

Luckily, all the steps of our programme are as applicable to ranges as to single products: analysis of the company's strengths may frequently lead to an idea for a whole range of products, which are then developed and perfected at the brand building stage. The final product + concept test, of course, must be organised in such a way that each product is separately tested, while at the same time obtaining reactions to the idea of the range as a whole; but this is a relatively minor complication.

Following the product + concept test, an item-by-item sales forecast can be produced; and at this stage a decision may be taken to reduce the number of items in the range, by killing off those where the forecast indicates the lowest sales estimates – for example, Gunpowder Green may be dropped from the intended range of speciality teas; or Siberia from the new range of holiday destinations.

But there may be another reason for reducing the number of items at this stage: this is to avoid a range consisting of items with too many close similarities. The ideal range provides the consumer with variety; to achieve this, each item should be significantly different from all the others. We have shown (see Chapter 4) how a sausage manufacturer reduced his different lines of sausages from twenty-two to thirteen, via a simple piece of research which demonstrated that several lines were so similar that the consumer was failing to distinguish between them. In the case of a new range of speciality teas, therefore, it is important to consider whether to include a single 'China' tea, or three called 'Jasmine', 'Lapsang Souchong', and 'Keemun'. Before adopting the latter course, the results of the product + concept test should be scrutinised for evidence that the consumer can distinguish between different China teas, in terms both of the concepts and of the products themselves.

In researching the new range of Iron Curtain package holidays, a high level of interest may have been obtained to the idea of both Odessa and Sebastopol as destinations. But does the consumer require a choice of two Black Sea resorts out of a range of only, say, ten destinations covering the whole of Russia and Eastern Europe? Were the respondents in the research who showed interest in Odessa the same people as those who wanted to go to Sebastopol? If so, there is a danger that our forecast of the popularity of each resort will be too high, as both are effectively competing for the same market segment.

3.2. Misuse of ranges

What are the advantages of a range? What is wrong with launching a male deodorant, an after-shave, a cologne, and a shower gel as separate and unconnected products – rather than grouping them into a range? One obvious feature of a range – especially in this case – is that it makes possible attractive gift multipacks. But to a marketing man the main advantage of a range is more fundamental: it allows the aggregation of marketing resources – especially advertising – behind a single brand. Whereas by itself, a package tour to Leningrad is unlikely to generate a sufficient marketing budget to justify advertising, a range of ten such holidays, under a single brand name, might well command a sizeable media budget. Twinings, the tea company, are unlikely to run an advertising campaign just for Earl Grey tea; but their whole range of speciality teas is, so to speak, a different kettle of fish.

Indeed, it can be dangerously tempting to force new products together into ranges, in order to reap the benefits of aggregated resources — even where no 'natural' range grouping exists. Recently a food company, testing a large number of new convenience food products, concluded that there were opportunities for traditional desserts such as apple crumble and rhubarb pie; they also identified a need for a number of main-meal centres in aluminium trays — such as lasagne, moussaka, shepherd's pie — for heating in the oven; while a separate part of their new product development programme had indicated that ready-prepared *Coquilles St Jacques* could be a winner. 'Wonderful', they said, 'we'll have an Oven Range.'

Now to the manufacturer, the fact that all these products require oven cooking may be the main element in common; but to a consumer it is probably the very last thing to consider. Who has heard anyone saying, 'Let's use the oven today. Now what shall we cook in it ... let me see. ...' Consumers are no more likely to think this way, than to say to themselves 'Let's eat international food tonight' (see page 116). In other words, the concept of the oven does not form a *natural* grouping for a range of food products. Typically, a consumer will decide upon how many courses to serve, what to make the centre of the main course, and where to buy it, before the question of whether or not to use the oven enters her head.

Equally wrong as a grouping, we believe, would be a range of hot beverages, under a single brand name, including tea, instant coffee, and drinking chocolate. But a marketing man from a country where hot beverages are not commonly drunk (if indeed there is such a country) may question this conclusion. After all, he would point out, all three of these beverages appeal to roughly the same target groups; many consumers drink all three regularly; they compete for the same drinking occasions; they are all imported substances; they are all drunk hot; they all have a long shelf life; and they sell through the same shops. But our visitor would not know that consumers rarely say to themselves, 'I'd like a beverage – I wonder what to have – I know, I'll have some tea.' In other words, a decision between tea, coffee and drinking chocolate is taken – almost subconsciously – long before any choice of brand or type. 'Beverage' is not a familiar consumer concept, and does not furnish a 'natural' basis for a range.

Another example from a slightly different field: a publisher recently brought out a set of some twenty smartly-bound volumes, entitled *The Nobel Prize Winners*. This consisted of extracts from the works of all those writers (about sixty in all, three per volume) who had won the Nobel Prize for Literature. A worthy undertaking, perhaps; but few readers, we would guess, select their books on the grounds that the author has a Nobel Prize. Besides, the writers, not surprisingly, were a heterogeneous bunch; and how many people are omnivorous enough to read Kipling, *and* André Gide, *and* John Steinbeck, *and* T.S. Eliot? If the number of remaindered sets we have seen in bookshops are any guide, our doubts on this venture have proved justified.

Equally, one would be doubtful about the chances of a range which included products for polishing and cleaning the car together with household products such as oven cleaner and silver polish. Here, of course, the target groups are very different; motorists tend to be men, whereas women still generally do the household cleaning, despite signs that strict role differentiation is breaking down. But even for a woman who runs her own car, this range would not make good sense: few women suddenly say to themselves: 'I think I'll do some cleaning – now what shall I clean?' Instead, they see that the car, or the oven, or the silver is dirty, and then set about cleaning it.

The guidelines for avoiding misconceived ranges are therefore:

(a) Ensure that each item in the range appeals to broadly the same target group.

(b) Check that the central idea behind the range reflects a familiar consumer concept, which fits in with consumers' decision-making processes.

3.3. The Decision Tree

Given the importance of understanding the decision-making processes which lead up to the purchase of a product, and the effect this can have on the grouping of products into ranges, we have pioneered a method of analysing qualitative research which we call the decision tree. At its simplest, it consists of asking consumers direct questions. Do they, for example, decide upon a type of floorcovering first, and then go to a shop specialising in carpets, or in vinyl floorcovering? Or do they look round some shops *before* making a decision on type of floorcovering? (Important to know, if a new brand of floorcoverings is planned, offering carpet and vinyl products as part of the same range.) Usually, the research concentrates upon recent purchasers. The interviewer attempts to reconstruct the thought-process which the consumer went through before arriving at a purchasing decision. Figure 8.1 shows an example of a decision tree in action, in the area of family feeding. It reveals many points of interest for a convenience food manufacturer attempting to launch new product ranges, or attempting to group existing products together into ranges, in order to achieve the benefits of aggregated resources. For example:

(a) The children, it seems, are often catered for and fed separately from the rest of the family. Thus a children's range could make sense.

(b) A clear distinction is drawn between a snack, which usually means relying on what is in the larder (e.g. bacon, eggs, or sausages), and a main meal, which usually entails shopping specially for meat (or possibly fish). Thus a range which included hamburgers (a snack product competing with sausages) and a prepared Hungarian goulash (an alternative to buying chops, steak, or a joint) would be totally wrong.

(c) 'Starters' and 'puddings' are, ironically, in much closer competition with each other than one might expect, in that both are a kind of 'extra'. Thus a range of convenience food products called 'Meal Extras', including both starters and sweets – crazy though the idea may sound – might just be viable.

4. Accentuate the negative

Faced with what looks like (or may even have been shown to be) a potentially damaging aspect of a new product concept, the natural instinct is to suppress the offending element – either by camouflaging it in the hope that no one will notice, or by changing the product in whatever way seems necessary. Where neither course is possible, the concept may even be abandoned altogether.

Often enough, such decisions (with the possible exception of the camouflage strategy, which is perilous) are sound and inevitable. But it is never a bad idea, before back-tracking, to take a long look at what seems to be a craggy and towering negative, on the off-chance that it might just be stood on its head and converted into a positive. Such things have, occasionally, been done.

Consider, for example, Vladivar Vodka. Normally, the last thing anyone would use as a selling argument for a vodka – especially one with a Russian name – would be that it was manufactured in, of all places, Warrington, Lancashire. The conventional wisdom would be to keep very quiet about such a shameful pedigree. So both the makers of Vladivar, and their advertising agency, deserve considerable credit for courage and imagination, in that far from concealing this apparent negative, they have proudly flaunted it aloft as the centerpiece of their campaign: 'Vladivar Vodka from Varrington – the greatest wodka in the vorld.' Entertaining, memorable – and certainly different.

Figure 8.1 A 'decision tree' for family feeding

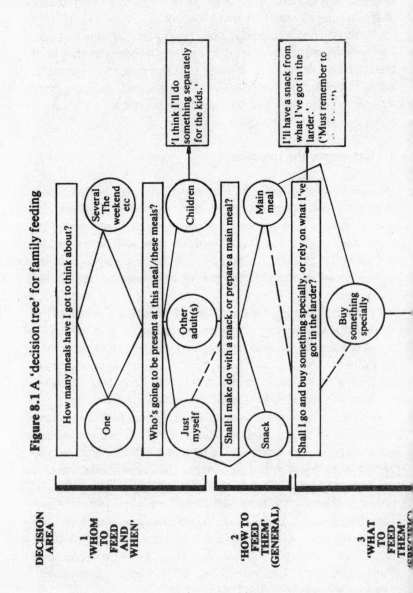

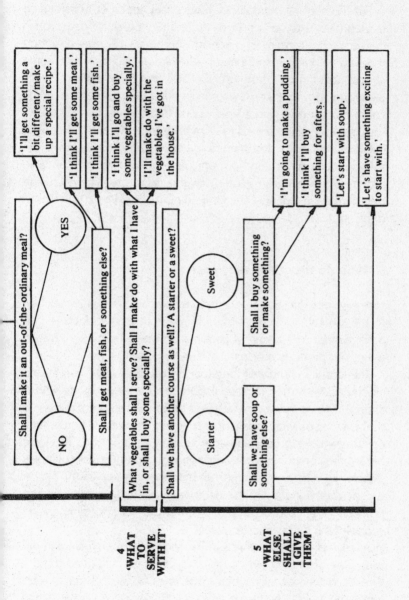

'I'll get something a bit different/make up a special recipe.'

'I think I'll get some meat.'

'I think I'll get some fish.'

'I think I'll go and buy some vegetables specially.'

'I'll make do with the vegetables I've got in the house.'

Shall I make it an out-of-the-ordinary meal?

YES

NO

Shall I get meat, fish, or something else?

What vegetables shall I serve? Shall I make do with what I have in, or shall I buy some specially?

Shall we have another course as well? A starter or a sweet?

Starter

Sweet

4 'WHAT TO SERVE WITH IT'

Shall we have soup or something else?

Shall I buy something or make something?

'I'm going to make a pudding.'

'I think I'll buy something for afters.'

'Let's start with soup.'

'Let's have something exciting to start with.'

5 'WHAT ELSE SHALL I GIVE THEM'

But the neatest example we have encountered of transforming a negative into a positive is a tale (possibly apocryphal) concerning a certain fish-canning company. It seems they had received a large consignment of salmon which – for some inexplicable reason – had turned white. There was nothing else at all wrong with it; it tasted excellent; but it was as white as prime cod. Colourants were not legally permitted for this food category; the company was resigned to selling the whole lot – at a loss – for cat food. But at the last minute someone had a brain-wave. The salmon was canned, and put on sale – at a premium – under a brand-name specially created for the occasion. And each can bore the proud legend: 'The Only Salmon That Won't Turn Pink in the Can'.

5. Who do they think they are?

One essential question to ask, before launching a new product on to the market, is: 'What's the self-image of this product?' Or, in other words: 'What kind of person is anyone who buys, or is seen using, our product, proclaiming him- or herself to be?'

The classic example of forgetting to ask this question is Strand cigarettes, with their famous slogan, 'You're never alone with a Strand'. The advertising, which was brilliantly executed, conveyed that even if you were lonely and excluded from all the parties, you could always find consolation in lighting up a Strand. The logic behind the campaign was evident enough: 'there are lots of lonely people, let's have a cigarette that is specially for them.' Fine – except that no one wants to be seen as being lonely; and to produce a packet of Strand was tantamount to announcing yourself as a social disaster area.

A less well-known instance of the same mistake occurred in the USA. One of the big baby food companies was intrigued to note that, at a time of falling birth rate, sales of their products were remaining steady, and even rising a little. There was no evidence that they were gaining brand-share from their competitors. The company investigated, and found that their products were increasingly being bought by elderly people for their own consumption – not surprisingly, given that (as mentioned earlier in this book) the dietary needs of the old are similar to those of infants, and that the baby foods came in single-person portions at a reasonable price.

Ah, thought the company, here was a market worth developing. Why not bring out a range specially aimed at these elderly consumers, with slightly less bland recipes (baby foods, for sound medical reasons, tend to be low on seasoning), under some such name as Fireside Dinners?

They did, and it flopped. Again, the self-image was totally wrong. Old people buying baby food could sustain the fiction that they were proud grandparents, part of a big happy family, buying for their new grandchild. But to buy a Fireside Dinner was to proclaim (to the other shoppers, to the check-out clerk): 'I'm a lonely old person, buying canned slop to eat in my solitary room.' In effect, the manufacturer was robbing consumers of their self-respect; naturally, they rejected his product.

6. The art of old product development

In most product fields, consumers welcome new products, and trial rates are high. But consumers do not like admitting that they have been persuaded to buy something new – it is bad for their self-image (see Section 5). On the whole, they would rather think of themselves as having *discovered* a product (perhaps one which has been around sometime – a local speciality in some remote part of the world), than as being in the market for a new brand. When Bacardi was first introduced to this country, it was a completely new drink to the British. It could have been positioned as a new invention in alcoholic drinks – a clear liquid with a mild taste of rum – and would probably have failed; few members of the cocktail set like to see themselves as guinea pigs for new product developers. Instead Bacardi was positioned as a 'discovery' from the West Indies – an exciting *traditional* drink now available in Britain, not a *new* drink at all. Thus the brand had a *pedigree*.

In many product fields we have found that a pedigree can make the difference between acceptance or rejection of a new product concept. We have seen (pp 97–8) how a range of boil-in-bag dinners was helped by the description 'bain-marie', thus helping consumers to see plastic bags in a new (or, rather, an old) light: a traditional cooking method brought up-to-date, rather than the invention of a plastic age. In the cigarette field, we have evidence that a brand will arouse greater interest among smokers if it appears to be a revival of a traditional brand, or is positioned as previously available only for export, or in another country – than if it is an obviously new brand, recently conceived and designed by an advertising agency.

As consumers become more sophisticated, they are developing an ability to 'see through' new product images. This is particularly apparent to anyone who has conducted group discussions over several years. These days a consumer will typically remark: 'Oh, I see the sort of image they're trying to create for this product' – a comment which would have been very rare ten years ago, unless a close relative of a copywriter or marketing expert had been recruited into the group in error. A classic case of consumers' ability to see through a firm's marketing thinking recently emerged from a study of high-quality teas on the continent of Europe. Brand X had been on the market for many years, with traditional though not very attractive pack designs; while brand Y, which was a relative newcomer to the market, came in very attractive (but also traditional-looking) packs. Brand Y was preferred to brand X in terms of its pack design, flavour, and name. Yet overall, consumers preferred to buy brand X. Why? Qualitative research revealed that the newer brand, although attractive and traditional in appearance, was not *genuine*. The pack, consumers explained, had obviously been designed to *look* old; whereas Brand X was obviously made by a genuinely old-established firm, as no-one would think of designing such a boring pack today!

A final example of the importance of a pedigree is also in the field of tea. In the course of experimenting with different combinations of herbal drinks, we hit upon the idea of mixing herbal infusions together with tea to create a new drink. Described like that, the idea sounded quite revolting to most tea drinkers. But we discovered that the idea was in fact not new; in Morocco and parts of Spain there is a tradition of combining herbs with tea: the drink used to be called Moorish Tea. Described and positioned this way — as a local speciality/discovery from the past — it aroused great interest in market research.

7. Do not over-estimate your competitors

Army training manuals, as we recall, made the dangerous assumption that the enemy was stupid; he could be relied upon to blunder into every trap. But, judging from the actions of marketing men in many companies, basic marketing training seems to encourage the opposite, yet equally dangerous view, that the competition is omniscient and all-powerful. This belief can take two forms: 'What's the point; if it were a good idea, the big boys would have done it already', or 'There's no need for us to research the idea — the opposition must have researched it when they launched'.

7.1. 'If it was any good, Heinz would have done it'

We have seen medium-sized companies, with excellent new product ideas, miss opportunities because they got cold feet. They could not believe that they were first with the idea; the absence of such a product on the market was, therefore, evidence that there was some frightful snag to the concept which they had failed to spot.

There are two main fallacies in their reasoning. First, the big companies will not necessarily have thought of the idea at all. There is much evidence to suggest that big companies are, on the whole, less innovative than small ones, though of course they may be very good at copying a small company's idea, and marketing it more efficiently. Secondly, if they *have* thought of the idea, they may have ruled it out only because it did not suit *their* requirements. A smaller company need not be deterred, just because the likely market for a new brand is too small to interest Heinz, Unilever, or ICI. Indeed, if the opportunity really is too small for the giants, the small company can hope to be left in peace to enjoy its additional turnover.

7.2. 'Let's ride in on the back of their research'

A new product development programme can often lead a company to enter a new market – new, that is, to the firm concerned – with a 'me-too' product, perhaps on the grounds that there is room to spare, and the market looks profitable. The marketing director briefs his technical department to come up with a product which will match the brand leader in physical performance; when they have achieved this, he launches it without further ado, on the grounds that what is good enough for the brand leader is good enough for him. 'They must have got the product right in their market research, so we'll be OK; why waste money duplicating their results?'

In fact, he could well be wrong on at least three counts. What his technical people define as 'product parity' may not be parity in consumers' terms – which is something only market research could tell him. Furthermore, the brand leader's product may be a poor one; and poor quality which is just tolerable in an established brand will not be acceptable in a new entrant on the market. Finally, the brand leader may *not* have carried out adequate research – he may just have been plain lucky, and one should not count on duplicating his luck.

7.3. Beware the defensive me-too

Nothing we have said, of course, should be interpreted as a recommendation to ignore the competition altogether. A major consideration in assessing a particular new product venture is the extent to which the competition (i) could, and (ii) would wish to challenge the new entrant with a defensive me-too. For example, Smith & Nephew, who created the market for slimmers' soups with their Nutriplan brand, had little defence against Heinz who brought out a range of low-calorie soups. (Strictly, a low-calorie soup – unlike Nutriplan – is not an adequate meal replacement, but that is too subtle to worry most slimmers.) Nutriplan could not quite match the prestige of the Heinz name; they were good at slimming products, but Heinz were good at soup, and that, in the end, was the decisive factor.

The ideal new brand, then, is one which the competition will find hard to copy, or which they will find not worth copying. Next best is a brand that will have time to create a sufficient franchise before the competition can enter the market.

7.4. And if there is no competition?

When a manufacturer is seeking to create a *new* market, he should look very carefully at the forecast he makes for his intended brand. He should remember that, to begin with, his brand and the market are identical. Therefore, if his forecast indicates that there is barely room for himself, he should beware. If he has to have nearly one hundred per cent brand share to survive, he should not launch, since *any* steal by a defensive me-too will destroy his profitability. The first manufacturer to launch a 'make-a-meal' (see page 31) could have foreseen this difficulty, if he had done a proper forecast.

8. Beware of over-broad targeting

Some manufacturers evince a dangerous inclination to test their new products among a far too broadly-defined target market. This is generally for one of two main reasons. First, because of the temptation to define one's target market as consisting of everybody; to aim at a minority segment, it is feared, will restrict the brand's potential. 'This is a food product, and everyone eats, don't they? So why risk missing anyone?' Yet a brand can only succeed if it is aimed precisely at *somebody*; to aim precisely at everybody is, clearly, impossible.

Babycham has always been very clearly targeted at young girls with little drinking experience. This has ensured the brand a definite personality; otherwise it would just be a fizzy perry in a little bottle. And it is unlikely that many people would buy an expensive, undefined fizzy perry in a little bottle. Yet branded as Babycham, the brand not only sells extremely profitably – it also sells to a lot of people *outside the target group*. Not having a personality leads to nothing; yet defining a tight target group does not necessarily restrict sales exclusively to that group.

The other motive for broad targeting is simply that the broader the research sample, the lower are the recruitment costs. This is evidently false economy, particularly since research costs are a very small proportion of the development costs of a new product; yet surprisingly often, such considerations are allowed to distort the research.

Take the following example. In France the market for frozen foods is less well developed than in other European countries. A new product development programme is under way, and two frozen food concepts have emerged as candidates for launch – a steak pie, and a savoury open flan. So a quantitative product + concept test on each concept is proposed. But frozen-food users represent only forty per cent of the population and only ten per cent of the population ever buy frozen meal centres, the remaining thirty per cent buying only frozen vegetables. The temptation to test the new products amongst frozen food users generally (or, still worse, among a sample of all housewives) is strong, but should be resisted.

Typically what happens is as follows: After scrutinising alternative cost quotations from the research agency, the manufacturer decides to conduct the tests amongst a sample of frozen-food buyers in general – a compromise between the cheapest solution (sampling all housewives), and the ideal (but much more expensive) procedure of recruiting buyers of frozen meal centres. The tests reveal that seven per cent of frozen-food buyers would definitely buy the pie and ten per cent would definitely buy the flan. A fairly encouraging result for the flan at first sight, but not significantly different, statistically, from the pie result – unless very large samples have been recruited (which is unlikely since cost saving was a factor in the original choice of research design).

In view of this dilemma, the company decides, after all, to conduct the 'proper' research: to repeat both the pie test and the flan test amongst the correct target group – buyers of frozen meal centres. To their surprise and delight, twenty-eight per cent of these consumers will definitely buy the flan, against only fifteen per cent for the pie – a decisive, significant, and encouraging result.

But should the company have been surprised? This sort of discrepancy between the two tests is not only possible, but very likely, as the table below indicates.

	Buyers of frozen food	Buyers of frozen meal centres	Buyers of frozen vegetables only
Incidence in population	40%	10%	30%
Definitely buy pie	7%	15%	4%
Definitely buy flan	10%	28%	4%

The two sets of figures are entirely compatible with each other. Amongst those who buy frozen vegetables but not frozen meal-centres, a large number are indifferent to both products; whereas the prime target group – those who really matter – strongly favour the flan. The moral: do not try to save research costs by testing amongst the wrong target market. This, of course, also goes for the brand building stage, when recruiting group discussions and depth interviews.

9. Consumer as art critic

In our research method, consumers are asked to respond to new product ideas, which, for convenience and realism, may be presented in mock advertisements (see Chapter 5). When consumers see advertisements, they love to play art critic – who does not? – but the researcher should not allow them to get carried away. The principle aim of the research is to elicit response to the *product* idea, not to the *advertisement*.

Some art criticism, of course, is inevitable, and can even be useful. If the appearance of the advertisement *confuses* the respondent, for example, that is worth knowing. But comments on the colour of the model's eyes are not helpful at this stage.

Nor should this point be forgotten at the final stage of development, when a real TV commercial has been prepared. In testing that commercial, the consumer should still be asked to assess the *product*, not the advertisement. Indeed, the test should not differ from the product + concept type of research described in our forecasting chapter. All we need to know is: does the commercial achieve the same 'definitely buy' response as the concept advertisement? We do not need to know whether the consumer *likes* our commercial, since there is absolutely no correlation between liking a commercial, and wanting to buy the product. A well-known American corsetry manufacturer once ran a commercial in the UK for one of its girdles. Sales rose sharply; yet research indicated that this was one of the most hated ads ever screened. Which probably shows that on balance it is better for a commercial to be obnoxious than ignored.

10. There is no such thing as an unimportant detail

One incidental consequence of the realistic representation of concepts (see Chapter 5) is that it requires attention to small detail. Which is all to the good, because small details matter. Often, they can make all the difference between success and failure.

A savoury snack manufacturer was working to develop a new crisp. He knew from market research that, although crisp buyers were generally pleased with existing crisps, they complained about the amount of fragments in the average packet. His answer was to produce a bigger crisp, which was slightly thicker, and so less liable to break at all, or to fragment into small pieces. Product testing with prototypes showed that his thicker crisp would be just as popular with consumers as the original variety (when unbroken). A mock advertisement was produced in which the new product was described as 'bigger, thicker, and crisper'. All of which was perfectly true, but the response from group discussions was unanimous – 'We don't want thick crisps, they're bound to be rubbery.'

The advertisement was changed by removing the single word 'thicker', and put back into research. 'Marvellous,' said the groups, 'when can we get some to try?' When they saw the product, they all said, 'Oh, I see, they're thicker, how sensible.' *Finding out* that the new product was thicker was quite reasonable; being *told* they were thicker raised unnecessary fears. One word was all it took.

Another example. Cavendish South African Sherry, already referred to (p. 61), was considered, after its launch in the UK, for both the

Dutch and German markets. In principle, the Cavendish format should do well in both countries. In Holland, sherry is considered to be a British, rather than a Spanish, drink, whilst in Germany sherry is largely unknown, but a British pedigree would be a useful way of introducing the drink. Therefore, the overtly British approach of the Cavendish branding should be right for both countries. But there was a legal snag. In EEC countries it is not permitted to call any product 'sherry' unless it comes from the Jerez district of Spain. (In the UK a special dispensation exists for the equivalent products from Cyprus, Australia, and South Africa.) What is worse, the regulations insist that the product is described, somewhere on the bottle, by its category name – *Likörwein*, or *Vin de Liquer*. Unfortunately the word liqueur, in most EEC languages, has connotations of extreme sweetness.

The problem was tackled by the use of an additional label on the bottle, which said – in very stark official-looking writing:

'Likörwein 17° (EWG-VERORDNUNG 816/71, Anlage 2)'
i.e. EEC Regulation 816/71, Clause 2.

In research, no one noticed this label at all, until it was pointed out. Then they remarked: 'Oh, I see, it's some Common Market regulation', and took no further notice – exactly the response we had hoped for. A small detail – but an important one.

In the UK, the Cavendish brand has a back label which describes the sherry-making process. For the research in Holland, we translated this into Dutch. To our surprise, this immediately created doubts amongst Dutch consumers that the product was not genuinely British, but rather some local imitation. In Germany, by contrast, the consumer wanted information about sherry – how it is made and when to drink it – but written in German, since not so many Germans know English. Printing the back label in English for Holland, but in German for Germany, is again a small detail – but an important one.

11. Where angels fear to tread

We have talked at length in this book about how companies can miss opportunities by doing too *much* market research: either too much expensive preliminary research (like Gap Analysis), or too much piecemeal research during the brand building stage. But we should not minimise the dangers of the opposite error – that of rushing on to the market far too quickly. A company may have an idea, check it out in a couple of group discussions, which respond enthusiastically; and launch. 'We must get on the market quickly,' they say, 'before the people down the road jump in.'

In case the reader needs further convincing, let us spell it out: group discussions are *not* predictive. They are very useful for eliciting the full range of responses to a new product idea, and alerting us to possible snags. But it simply is not possible to devise meaningful forecasts from group discussions. Eight respondents in a room together collude; their response to anything so specific as, 'Would you buy this brand?' will be a *group* answer. Recently we researched the idea of a clothes freshener – for use between dry cleans, to freshen up clothes hanging in the wardrobe. 'Horrible!' was the group answer; yet when the product was tested quantitatively, a sizeable number of respondents said they would definitely buy. An example of the opposite discrepancy occured over the idea of a special product for cleaning lavatory seats. In groups, the product was greeted with enormous enthusiasm (possibly a further example of Group Approved Sentiments – see pp 111–12); but when it was tested quantitatively, the number who said they would buy it was disappointingly low.

12. 'Why wasn't I consulted?'

The true figures would be impossible to establish, but it is our guess that, of all the new products that fail, at least twenty-five per cent do so not for any external reasons in the market, but through internal sabotage. By which we do not mean simple mismanagement, or common-or-garden incompetence (though these also take their toll) – but deliberate action within a company against a particular new product.

To be fair, 'deliberate action' is perhaps slightly overstating the case. Far more common is deliberate *inaction* – undermining a product by doing as little as possible towards its success or, in the words of the poet:

> 'Thou shalt not kill – but need'st not strive
> Officiously to keep alive.'

The reasons for such calculated not-striving are many; but most of them, we believe, come down to a lack of involvement – a feeling that, 'This is someone else's product, not mine'. From there, it is a short step to indifference, or downright hostility.

Every company has its share of office politics, of course; putting the skids under X's new product may well be seen as a promising way of putting the skids under X. Such plotting – fortunately – is outside the scope of this book. But the problems of individual non-involvement are perhaps more easy to deal with; in many cases, we believe, they come down to a question of good internal communications.

One thing most of us cannot take is to be ignored. We would rather be disagreed with, even attacked, than overlooked. Better that our advice should be asked, and then rejected, than that no one should ask our advice at all. Above all, we want to be kept informed. 'No one ever tells me anything!' is a pathetic cry – the cry of wounded self-respect.

At the outset of every new product development project, therefore, we have found it pays dividends to tell everybody whose cooperation is likely to be needed what is going on – at least in broad terms – and to solicit their advice. At best, we may well learn something of value; at worst, comments can be ignored, or paid lip-service. But either way, we have started to create a sense of identification – to make people feel that this is to some extent 'their' project.

The danger of not keeping everyone informed was brought home to us quite early in our product development career. We had been called in by a food laboratory specialising in dairy products, with links to various food marketing companies around Europe. The laboratory wanted our help in developing new kinds of natural (i.e. non-processed) cheese. ('Invented' natural cheeses may sound anomalous, but in fact many cheeses *are* deliberately invented, rather than evolved through generations of peasant wisdom. Boursin is a successful recent example.) We came up with twenty or so promising concepts; the laboratory produced some delicious samples; and we embarked on research in several countries.

At this stage, none of the marketing companies knew what we were doing. This was deliberate policy on the part of the laboratory, and we, in our ignorance, did not question their decision. The research results were encouraging: several of the new cheeses proved highly popular and – according to our market estimates – could well have become successful brands all over Europe. A grand meeting was therefore arranged, at which these auspicious findings could be presented to the representatives of all the marketing companies.

It was a most embarrassing meeting. The assembled marketing directors and brand managers sat round a vast table, and listened in total silence while the laboratory heads proudly outlined the initiative they had taken. We then presented our findings; the silence deepened. The head of the laboratory summed up, in glowingly optimistic terms; still his audience remained mute. He concluded – and asked for comments.

The storm broke.

Luckily (for us, at least) most of the fury was directed at the laboratory heads, not at us. We cowered in our chairs while verbal volleys and cannonades hurtled over our heads. 'Who authorised …?' 'Why weren't we told …?' 'Figures already available …' 'Local marketing facts overlooked …' 'Duplication of effort …' 'Could have told you …' 'If anyone had bothered to ask ME …'

Most furious of all was the representative of one local company, who seemed to take it as a direct personal insult that some of the research had been carried out in *his* country, without his knowledge.

In the end, of course, everyone calmed down, and even admitted, grudgingly, that some of the work we had done was not totally without value, and could perhaps be further developed. But we all knew that nothing more would really come of it; the project was dead. By their insistence on secrecy, the laboratory had alienated all those whose cooperation would be needed to advance the work; no one in any of the marketing companies could ever come to regard any part of the project as being 'his'. And several promising new product concepts were thus strangled at birth.

'Keep everyone informed' is, we realise, a counsel of perfection. In some highly competitive markets (cigarettes, for example) secrecy is considered vital; the fewer people know of a new project, the better. Or – especially in large companies – the sheer numbers involved may make full communication impossible.

A fine distinction needs to be drawn, too, between 'Keep everyone informed' and 'Keep everyone involved'. Committees, in our view, are the death of effective new product development. Nothing slows progress, muddles objectives, and inflates costs so inexorably as having to involve and consult large numbers of people at each stage of a project.

The ideal, if it can be achieved, is to inform the maximum number of people, and involve the minimum. Solicit everybody's opinion before the project starts; circulate the occasional progress report while it continues; present the final results at a grand meeting, paying graceful tribute to each person's invaluable contribution. Such basic diplomacy may seem elementary, even naive, but it can do a lot to smooth the path of a new product within a company, and it is surprisingly often neglected.

Conclusion

A matter of confidence

We have referred earlier (pp 144–6) to the danger of a new product development programme generating its own unstoppable momentum, but we suspect that such cases are exceptional. Far more often, it is the opposite problem that has to be overcome in getting a new product on the market – that of sheer inertia. Inertia both internal ('Production lines are overloaded', 'The salesforce won't wear it') and external, especially from the trade ('Not *another* new brand!' 'I can't spare any more facings'). Overcoming this kind of resistance requires energy and perseverance, but above all it requires confidence. Those not committed to a brand will always be able to produce a hundred and one reasons why life would be better without it. They will only be persuaded if the marketing team really believes in what it is doing. Lack of conviction shows through all too clearly.

Blind faith would be absurd. But we have tried to show in this book how it is possible to build a brand in which a company can have total confidence – on the most rational and demonstrable grounds. Systematic analysis of opportunities, painstaking brand building through flexible research, the final forecasting of sales – these provide all the proof needed to foster confidence within the company, and furnish logical arguments for optimism to the trade. 'We believe in this product – and here's cogent evidence *why* we believe in it' is a powerful line of persuasion.

Too many companies simply go through the motions, treating new product development as a pious exercise, or as a gamble. They do not really believe there is much chance of success; and their lack of confidence becomes a self-fulfilling prophecy, ensuring failure. Without such confidence, of course, no system (ours or anybody else's) can do much to help. But the combination of a systematic approach, imaginatively and intelligently used, and the rational confidence that such a system can engender, will, if not guarantee success (nothing, after all, can do *that*), certainly increase the chances of it many times over.

Index